Pescatarian Paradise

Creative fish dishes – full of flavour for every day and for special occasions

Author proceeds from this book will be donated to
Cancer Research UK, to support their vision to bring
forward the day when all cancers are cured.

Alison Howe

Matador
Unit E2 Airfield Business Park,
Harrison Road, Market Harborough,
Leicestershire. LE16 7UL
Tel: 0116 2792299
Email: books@troubador.co.uk
Web: www.troubador.co.uk/matador
Twitter: @matadorbooks

ISBN 978 1803132 945

British Library Cataloguing in Publication Data.
A catalogue record for this book is available from the British Library.

Printed and bound by CPI Group (UK) Ltd, Croydon, CR0 4YY
Typeset in 11pt Palatino by Troubador Publishing Ltd, Leicester, UK

Matador is an imprint of Troubador Publishing Ltd

Introduction

I am an enthusiastic home cook and this recipe book reflects a lifetime's interest in food. As a student I worked at weekends for a friend who was a professional chef. I was thrown in at the deep end, and I had to quickly learn essential cooking techniques and, importantly, how to maximise the flavour of food. I have undertaken several advanced cookery courses which gave me the confidence to develop my culinary style and to create new dishes. I was fortunate to travel widely during my career, giving me the opportunity to taste many national and regional dishes which I then incorporated into my own cooking style, particularly the use of herbs and spices to enhance flavour.

Seven years ago, my partner and I 'escaped to the countryside' in West Sussex, and I found that by using local suppliers, who are passionate about what they grow and sell, I had arrived in a cook's paradise! This included Johnson's Enterprises, a family-run fish merchants, who supply wonderfully fresh, locally caught seafood. I soon became a pescatarian as a lifestyle choice and an enthusiastic fish cook. I started to create new ways to cook the catch of the day, basing these recipes both on modern British cooking techniques and flavours, and those which had inspired me during my visits to Italy, Spain, France and North America. There is a significant focus on SE Asian flavours and cooking preparation, which I have always enjoyed.

Over the Covid-19 lockdown, I decided that it was an ideal opportunity to capture these dishes in a fish cookery book. I wanted to offer creative recipes which can be reliably and quickly achieved using fish which is readily available at local fishmongers and supermarkets. For the most part these dishes will not take more than thirty to forty minutes to cook, but there are some recipes for special occasions which will take longer – they are well worth the invested time and effort.

This is more of a cook's notebook, rather than a traditional cookery book. Each of the recipes includes helpful 'tips' based on my own experiences of cooking these dishes. This will ensure that you succeed the first time you try one of these new recipes!

Each recipe has an accompanying photograph. These were taken at home, as the dishes were cooked for family meals and are realistic illustrations of what you can expect to achieve yourself!

I hope that this book inspires you to create your own personal signature fish dishes. Pescatarian cooking is delicious, nutritious, quick to cook and very versatile – I hope that this informal approach will encourage you to experiment and to extend your own repertoire.

Acknowledgements

I could never have undertaken this ambitious project on my own, and I would like to thank those who have so generously given their time and support along the way.

Firstly, my partner Richard Hunt has been hugely supportive of the concept of writing this book and has encouraged me at every stage of its development. He has enthusiastically sampled all the dishes and provided excellent input regarding how to perfect them. Also, he has diligently photographed all the dishes I have cooked, and solved the considerable IT challenges that came with undertaking the practicalities of this project.

I would also like to thank Andrew Johnson, his daughter Katie and the wonderful team at Johnson's Enterprises, for supplying and preparing the delicious fish used to create these recipes and photographs. This family-run mobile seafood business, covering Hampshire and West Sussex, provides locally caught fish. They are passionate about the quality of the produce that they supply, and their experience in how to prepare and cook fish has been invaluable.

Blackdown Printers, especially Philip Jackson and Helen Taylor, provided very helpful advice on ensuring the photographs were optimised for printing and undertook meticulous preparation of the images prior to printing.

I would also like to thank some special friends who offered to test run my recipes and provided excellent, constructive suggestions on how I could make improvements. Thank you to Ruth Scudamore, Christine Musgrove, Lisa McConkey and Christine Pounder. Thanks also to Jane Short for her helpful advice regarding the design and presentation of the book.

In writing this book I wanted to make a positive contribution to supporting Cancer Research UK with their important work to find new ways to prevent, diagnose and treat cancer. If you have bought this book, or you are browsing through it and are considering purchasing it, I would like to thank you most sincerely as the author proceeds will be donated to Cancer Research UK for their work to help beat cancer. This is an opportunity for you to be a part of this important endeavour.

I would like to recognise the encouragement, help and advice provided by Cancer Research UK, especially Claire Moore and Akhil Anand.

A word about the use of alcohol and processed red meat in these recipes

Some of the recipes use wine and small amounts of processed meat such as bacon and chorizo. Although these items can be enjoyed occasionally, they should not make up the bigger part of our diet. Cancer Research UK recommends cutting down on alcohol and processed meat.

Contents

Techniques for Successful Fish Cookery

As mentioned in the introduction, my cookery skills are largely self-taught. Through a process of experimentation with new dishes, I have developed some helpful tips regarding techniques to enhance the subtle flavours of fish and how to cook delicious dishes reliably and quickly.

I'd like to pass this information on to you (see below) so you can keep it in mind as you cook the recipes in this book. Hopefully, you will soon be adding your own ideas to improve the dishes and create your own recipes!

You will find that there are tips inserted in most the of the recipes and these are specific to the dish. The techniques below can be applied to most recipes.

- **Buy the freshest fish that you can find.** If you don't live near an independent fishmonger, I suggest that you go to the website of the National Federation of Fishmongers. There's a tab where you can find the details of fishmongers in your region, who will enable you to source the range of fish that I have used in this book and will provide helpful advice on its preparation. Also, look online for fishmongers in your area – there are more than you may be aware of. Waitrose, Sainsbury's and Morrison's have in-store fish counters, and most supermarkets sell prepared fresh fish in a dedicated area of the store.

- **If freezing fish, try to remove as much air as possible from the packaging** – vacuum sealing is best. A couple of fish which are much better eaten fresh are mackerel and lobster, but most of the other fish used in this book will be fine in a freezer for a period of up to two months. When thawing the fish, it is best to do this slowly. Place the fish in the fridge overnight and then allow it to come to room temperature for one to two hours before use. It is important that the thickest portion of the fish is fully thawed because, otherwise, it will take longer to cook, and the rest of the fish will be overcooked.

- **Recipes should aim to enhance the flavour of the fish.** I have tried to follow this throughout the book, and have used a wide range of herbs and spices to highlight the flavour of the fish.

- **The cooking temperature and duration is critical for successful fish dishes.** When fish is heated the flesh releases liquid. If the internal temperature is too high, or the cooking period prolonged, too much of this fluid is lost and the fish becomes dry and loses its elasticity. So, taking care with the cooking time and temperature is key for a tender and tasty dish.

- **Cooking thermometers are not expensive and are widely available online.** Measuring the core temperature of fish *at its thickest point* is the simplest, and the most accurate, way to ensure your fish dishes are perfectly cooked. Here are the internal temperature ranges for cooking different fish – essentially, if you aim for 50°C for fish and 45°C for shellfish, you will be successful!

  - White fish: 52°C
  - Halibut: 48–50°C
  - Flatfish: 50–52°C
  - Monkfish: 47–58°C
  - Salmon: 48–52°C
  - Tuna: 31°C – pink centre
  - Mussels: 45°C
  - Lobster: 45°C

  If you haven't got a thermometer, then these are useful tips to gauge when fish is cooked:

  - Fish isn't sufficiently cooked if the flesh is transparent, and the flakes adhere.
  - Fish is done when it is opaque and moist and there's a bit in the middle of the fillet that is slightly transparent, like mother-of-pearl. This will cook with the residual heat.
  - Fish is overcooked if it is one opaque colour all the way through. It will be dry and stringy.
  - Mussels, oysters: when the shells (previously closed) open

- **Take your fish out of the fridge for <u>at least</u> fifteen minutes ahead of cooking.** This allows it to come to room temperature and reduces the cooking time. If you can allow more time than this, that will be even better. At this time, season the fish with salt and pepper and lemon/lime juice, and for spicy dishes add a sprinkle of red chilli seeds for added warmth of flavour. The individual recipes provide more guidance on this.

Some tips on frying fish

Frying fish adds flavour. Here are some ways to optimise the outcome:

- **The cooking temperature of the oil is critical:** if it is too high the fish will burn, but if it is too low the fish will release fluids and boil rather than fry to a nice crispy, golden surface (between 170–180°C is ideal for most fish). For pan-frying, use a refined cooking oil such as canola, vegetable, corn or sunflower oil.

- **The fish should be completely dry** on the surface when you put it in the frying pan. Use paper towel to blot the fish and then dust it with a little plain flour if there is still excess fluid.

- **Use a thick-bottomed frying pan** which can go directly into the oven for finishing off dishes.

- **Butter or high-quality cooking oil?** I use cooking oil (see above) as butter becomes dark brown during the cooking. If I want to get a richer taste, I add a little butter for basting at the end.

- **Don't overload the frying pan** – the temperature will drop; the liquid that the fish produces will not evaporate; and it will be boiled instead of fried. If you have more fish than pans, slightly undercook the fish on one side, place them on a dish in a preheated oven at about 120°C. Then, just ahead of serving, place the fish back in the pan, the undercooked side in contact with the pan surface, and complete the cooking/reheating (this needs to be very quick).

- **To prevent the fish sticking to the pan** – shake the pan slightly in the first few seconds so the fish browns but does not stick.

- **Approximate frying times:** thin fillets – one to two minutes per side; thick fillets and cutlets – three to five minutes per side. If the fish surface becomes too brown, place the whole pan in a preheated oven (180°C) for a couple of minutes to finish off.

Some tips on baking fish

I find that fatty fish are best for baking – for instance salmon fillets, mackerel and fish cooked whole:

- **For salmon fillets:** firstly, marinade the salmon fillets in salt, pepper and lemon juice for about fifteen minutes to allow the fish to get to room temperature (reduces the cooking time). Carefully dry the fish. Preheat the oven to 200°C. Butter an open dish and place the salmon skin side down on it. Add any herbs/flavourings you are using on the upper surface of the fish and some knobs of butter (see the individual recipes).

Cook for about six minutes, then check cooking progress every two minutes. If using a thermometer (recommended), the fish is done when the internal temperature is 50°C at the thickest part. If judging by eye, the fish is done when there's a bit in the middle of the flakes that is slightly transparent, like mother-of-pearl. This will cook with the residual heat. Also, using the tip of a small knife, delicately separate out two flakes of flesh in a thick portion of the fish – if it separates easily, the fish is cooked.

- **For medium-sized whole fish:** marinade the fish in lemon juice, salt and pepper for at least ten minutes on either side. Carefully dry the fish. Preheat the oven to 200°C. Butter the cooking dish and oil (extra virgin olive oil) and season the outer surfaces of the fish. Open out the underside flaps of the fish and use these to prop it into a 'swimming position' on the cooking dish. Place in the oven and cook for twenty minutes. Check at one-minute intervals thereafter until cooked – see above for tips to gauge this.

Some tips on grilling fish (this is based on an electric grill inside the oven)

I find that grilling fish is fast and predictable for the most part, but it is not suitable for all seafood. As before, take your fish out of the fridge about fifteen minutes before cooking so it comes up to room temperature. During that time, marinade it in lemon/lime juice and seasoning. Preheat the grill to 200°C. Take out the grill pan and line the rack with tinfoil, brushed with olive oil (which withstands grilling better than when used for frying). Pat the fish dry with a paper towel and place on the grill – skin side down. Brush on any flavourings etc – this is explained within the recipes. When the grill is up to temperature, slide in the grill pan so it is four to five inches below the hot grill elements. Cook for four minutes on one side and then flip the fish over, using a long spatula, and cook for another two to three minutes.

These cooking instructions are quite general – the more detailed descriptions are given within each recipe.

A word about seasoning

I have aimed to use seasonings including garlic, chillies, ginger, dill, tarragon and other herbs etc to appeal to the 'average' palate. However, you might want to adjust the suggested amounts according to your own preferences.

I have also provided cooking times which should work well. However, exact times will be influenced by the thickness of the fish you are using, the time it has been out of the fridge prior to cooking and the heat generated by your oven. So, please do use the cooking times I've stated as a predictable guide, but check whether your dish is optimally cooked using a cooking thermometer or one of the more visual recommendations described above.

Store Cupboard

In the ingredients list for the individual recipes, I reference herbs, flavourings and cooking utensils that you may not have to hand in your store cupboard. The majority are widely available at supermarkets or online. I thought it would be helpful to provide a list of these items below, indicating my preferred brands and where you can source them. I haven't provided exhaustive lists of where these items can be obtained – rather, I have concentrated on three main supermarkets (Sainsbury's, Tesco and Waitrose) and a couple of online sources.

Item	Availability
Artichoke cream / paste	*Seggiano* or *Biona Organic*: Amazon; Waitrose Cook's Ingredients
Artichokes in oil	Amazon, Sainsbury's, Tesco, Waitrose
Asparagus cream	*Biona Organic*: Amazon
Anchovy fillets, marinated	Amazon, Sainsbury's, Tesco, Waitrose
Choux pastry buns, cocktail-sized and small pastry tartlets	Food Angles at foodangles.com: Pidy's brand
Sweet chilli sauce	*Blue Dragon*: Amazon, Sainsbury's, Tesco, Waitrose
Crab meat: fresh, white or mixed brown and white	Best to source from your fishmonger, or failing that try Sainsbury's, Waitrose or Morrisons
Croustades, mini size for cocktails	*Rahms*: Amazon, Sainsbury's, Waitrose
Cooking thermometers	Amazon, John Lewis, Lakeland
Eel, smoked	Best to source from your fishmonger, or try *Dukeshillham.co.uk*
Fishmongers selling a wide range of fresh fish, near you	Regional lists are available throughout the UK from the *National Federation of Fishmongers* (www.Fishmongersfederation.co.uk). Also, search online for fishmongers near you. The Fish Society provides excellent online fish, next day
Thai fish sauce	*Blue Dragon*: Sainsbury's, Tesco, Waitrose Cook's Ingredients

Hot gooseberry chutney	*Wilkin & Sons Ltd:* Amazon, Sainsbury's, Tesco, Waitrose stock another manufacturer
Hollandaise sauce	*Maille*: Amazon, Sainsbury's, Tesco, Waitrose
Lemongrass puree	*Chop*: Amazon, Sainsbury's, Tesco, Waitrose
Pastry tartlet cases for cocktails	Food Angles at foodangles.com
Palm sugar	Amazon, Sainsbury's, Tesco, Waitrose
Pesto, basil	*Sacla Classic Basil Pesto*: Amazon, Sainsbury's, Tesco, Waitrose
Pesto truffle	*Crema di funghi e tartufo bianco: Terra Sanpietrese* – other brands are available, but this has a great taste. Order online from manufacturer
Pesto, truffle and artichoke	*Belazu:* Amazon, Sainsbury's, Tesco, Waitrose
Smoked salmon – *long cut*	Best to source from your fishmonger, or failing that try Ocado, Severn Wye or Waitrose
Saltine crackers	*Premium, Nabisco*: Amazon
Steamer, stainless steel fan	Amazon, John Lewis
Soy sauce, Japanese (a low-salt version is available)	*Kikkoman*: Amazon, Sainsbury's, Tesco, Waitrose
Smoked garlic paste	*Bart or Chop*: Amazon, Sainsbury's, Tesco, Waitrose
Stock cubes/concentrated stock pots (fish flavour)	*Knorr* (preferred brand): widely available
Thai basil leaves, fresh	Sainsbury's, Tesco, Waitrose
Tempura mix	Amazon, Sainsbury's, Tesco, Waitrose
Yuzu citrus seasoning	Amazon, Tesco, Waitrose

Delicious, Quick-to-Prepare Canapés

Crispy fried fresh sage leaves with anchovies

This is an unusual starter – it's easy to prepare and the taste really pops – good for people who are a little more adventurous in their food choices.

Ingredients

Allow for 2–3 marinated anchovy fillets per canape. (for supplier see Store Cupboard, **page 12**)

2 fresh sage leaves per canape – select the larger leaves

Tempura batter mix (for supplier see Store Cupboard, **page 12**)

2–3 tbs plain flour

Cooking oil for pan-frying

Smoked paprika powder

Cooking instructions

1. Select well-shaped anchovy fillets, appropriate for the size of the fresh sage leaves. (*Tip: before cooking, wash the anchovies in milk to remove excess oil and salt.*) Dry carefully between 2 sheets of paper towel.

2. Make a parcel by laying 1–2 anchovy fillets between 2 sage leaves.

3. Make the tempura batter according to the packet instructions. (*Tip: aim for a light coating consistency, like double cream. Using ice cold sparkling water to mix the batter helps achieve this.*) Do this just before cooking to ensure crispy tempura.

4. Dust the anchovy and sage parcel with plain flour and then, holding one end of the parcel with kitchen tweezers, pass through the tempura mix so it is evenly, but thinly, coated.

5. Heat cooking oil in a heavy-bottomed, non-stick frying pan. When sizzling, drop in the anchovy parcels. Cook for about 30 seconds to 1 minute on each side until they are golden brown on the outside.

6. Dust with smoked paprika powder.

7. Drain on a paper towel.

Serving suggestions and accompaniments

Serve immediately so the parcels are warm when eaten. Olives (particularly green ones stuffed with anchovies or garlic), or whole roasted almonds, go well with this.

Crab and mango in pastry choux buns

This is easy to prepare, and the taste of the crab goes very well with the sweetness of the mango. It is served in a bite-sized choux pastry bun, which can be eaten in one tasty mouthful.

Makes about 10 choux buns

Ingredients

A box of ready-to-use, cocktail-sized choux pastry buns. These can be purchased online ahead of time. (*Tip: try Pidy's brand – see Store Cupboard, page 12.*)

75g white crab meat

Juice and zest of ½ lime

1tbs thick natural Greek yogurt

2 spring onions finely chopped (white part only)

½ tsp cayenne pepper

Salt and pepper

1 mango (not overripe)

Juice ½ lime

Coriander leaves to decorate

Cooking instructions

1. Cut the tops off the choux buns and check that they will be stable on a plate – if not, carefully shave off the bottom of each to make a flat surface. Don't cut through the bottom though, or you will lose the filling!

2. Stir together the crab meat, juice and zest of lime, yogurt, spring onions, cayenne. Season with salt and pepper to taste. Refrigerate until needed.

3. Place half the mango into a small food processor and add the juice of ¼ of a lime. Blitz to a puree. Place in the fridge. Cut the other half of the mango into very small cubes and pour on the juice from the remaining lime.

4. Place a little of the mango puree in the bottom of each choux case. Then spoon the crab mix into the tartlet cases and top with a few cubes of the diced mango and decorate with coriander leaves.

5. Eat soon after assembling.

Prawn cocktail served in canapé-sized pastry tartlets

This is an attractive way to jazz up a dish of canapés.
The prawn cocktail is served in small tartlet pastry cases.

Serves 4

Ingredients

Either buy ready-made cocktail pastry tartlet cases (available online – see Store Cupboard, **page 12**, for details) or make some from ready-made shortcrust pastry and a well-buttered, canapé-sized tartlet baking tray.

200g bag of good-quality frozen, cold-water prawns.

Juice ¼ lemon

Salt and pepper

Marie Rose sauce:

3 tbs good-quality, thick mayonnaise

1 tbs tomato ketchup

¼ tsp Worcestershire sauce

2 dashes Tabasco

Juice ¼ lemon

Salt and pepper

Sprigs of flat-leaf parsley

Cooking instructions

1. Thaw the cold-water prawns, and then marinade for 15 minutes in lemon juice and salt and pepper. Then drain and dry carefully on a paper towel.

2. If making the tartlet pastry cases, roll the pastry as thin as you can – you want to emphasise the taste of the filling. Cook the tartlets for about 10 mins at 180°C, and then cool on a rack before filling.

3. Combine all the ingredients for the Marie Rose sauce and season. Add the prawns.

4. Just ahead of serving, place the prawns into the tartlet cases. Garnish with a leaf of parsley.

Smoked eel on rye bread

I got a taste for smoked eel when I spent some years working in Scandinavia.
Smoked eel was very popular, and this is one of the dishes I liked the best.

Serves 4–6

Ingredients

8 long-cut strips of smoked eel – get the best quality you can and try to avoid oily brands. If smoked eel is not available, smoked salmon can be substituted

1 finely chopped red onion

6 small capers, sliced

½ tsp good-quality white wine vinegar

3–4 sprigs of dill, chopped

½ tsp sugar

Salt and pepper

4–6 pieces of brown rye bread

2 tsp horseradish cream

1–2 tbs full-fat crème fraiche

4 hard-boiled quails' eggs

Grated zest ½ lemon

Cooking instructions

1. Put the finely chopped red onion and capers in a bowl and add vinegar, dill, sugar, salt and pepper and mix. Marinade for about 30 minutes. Then drain off any excess juices.

2. Cut the rye bread into canapé-sized pieces.

3. Lay the eel strips on a paper towel to drain off excess oil. Season with course ground black pepper.

4. Cut the eel to fit the rye bread portions.

5. Mix the horseradish with the crème fraiche. Assemble canapés by spreading a little of the horseradish cream on the rye bread. Then place on a thin layer of the onion, caper and dill mix. Finally, carefully position the eel and gently press down each canapé.

6. Dress with a small amount of crème fraiche, a slice of hard boiled (quail's) egg, a sprig of dill and some lemon zest.

Serving suggestions and accompaniments

Serve with gherkins and salted roast nuts.

Thai prawn balls on cocktail sticks

These are always very popular. The raw ingredients can be made well ahead of time,
but once they are cooked, they do need to be eaten while warm.

Serves 4

Ingredients

200g bag uncooked, high-quality cold-water prawns

2 cloves of garlic, finely chopped

Lemongrass puree (see Store Cupboard, **page 12**, for suppliers)

1–2 inches fresh ginger, peeled and grated

½ red chilli, deseeded, chopped finely

2 spring onions, finely chopped

2–3 Thai basil leaves, remove the leaves from the stalks and chop finely

½–1 tbs sweet chilli sauce (Blue Dragon – for suppliers see Store Cupboard, **page 12**)

Juice of 1 lime and zest of ½ lime

1 tsp fish sauce

1 beaten medium-sized egg

1–2 tbs unsweetened desiccated coconut

5 sprigs coriander, remove the leaves from the stalks and chop

1 tbs plain flour

Cooking oil for pan-frying

Cooking instructions

1. Open the bag of prawns and place on paper towel to drain thoroughly.

2. Blitz the garlic, lemongrass puree, grated ginger, red chilli, spring onions, Thai basil leaves, sweet chilli sauce, lime juice and zest and fish sauce in a food blender – do not overprocess.

3. Add the beaten egg and the desiccated coconut – this provides flavour and brings the mixture into a consistency for making balls. (*Tip: add the coconut 1 tbs at a time until the mixture can be formed into balls.*) Lastly, mix in the chopped coriander.

4. Form the mixture into bite-sized balls, roll in plain flour and fry in hot cooking oil in a heavy, non-stick skillet. Take care not to overcook – the balls tend to char on the outside quite quickly.

5. Drain on a paper towel.

6. Serve on cocktail sticks with a dipping sauce of hot, sweet chilli.

Smoked salmon and horseradish pinwheels

This is a tasty, easy-to-make, standby canapé and makes a change from smoked salmon on brown bread or baked blini. I always make more than I think will be needed as they are always very popular.

Makes enough for 6 people, assuming other canapés will be offered

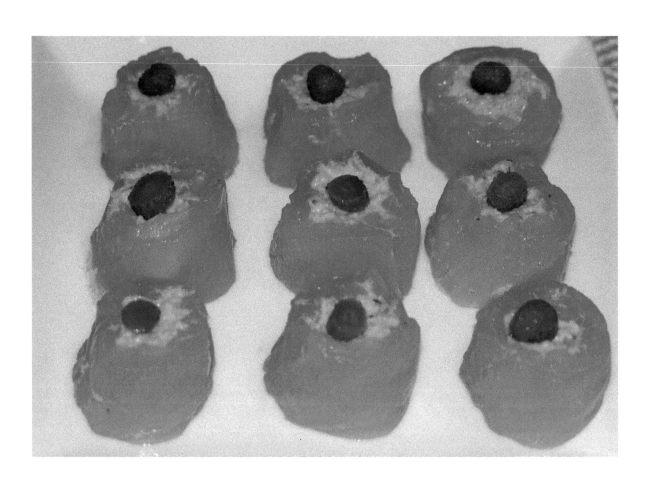

Ingredients

120g long-cut smoked salmon (for suppliers see Store Cupboard, **page 12**)

1 tbs horseradish sauce

1 tbs good-quality, thick, mayonnaise

Salmon pate filling:

150g smoked salmon, coarsely chopped (*tip: offcuts will work*)

100g full-fat cream cheese

Zest of 1 lemon and grated zest of ½ lemon

4 sprigs fresh dill, chopped

Cooking instructions

1. Place all the ingredients for the salmon pate into a food processor and blitz. However, take care not to overdo and to retain some of the texture in the pate. Check the seasoning as smoked salmon can vary greatly in its saltiness. Chill for 30 minutes.

2. Lay out the long strips of smoked salmon. Mix the horseradish sauce and the mayonnaise and with the back of a teaspoon spread over one side of the salmon strips. Then, spread the salmon pate evenly over the strips. (*Tip: avoid putting on too much pate as rolling up the salmon will be difficult.*)

3. Roll up the salmon strips like a Swiss roll. (*Tip: these need to be quite tight, so the rolls stay in shape.*) Tightly wrap each salmon roll in cling film. Chill for at least 1 hour.

4. Remove the cling film. Using a very sharp knife, cut the rolls crosswise to form bite-sized portions. Garnish with dill and place in the fridge until required.

Gentleman's Relish palmiers

These are a very tasty canapés which can be made in advance and then placed in the deep freeze until needed. Gentleman's Relish is a spicy anchovy paste, the recipe of which dates back to 1828 and is a carefully guarded secret. It is widely available in supermarkets – and sometimes it is sold with two other variations: one based on smoked salmon and the other on mackerel, both of which work well for this recipe.

Makes enough for 12-15 canapés, depending on the size you make them

Ingredients

320g pack of ready-made and pre-rolled all butter puff pastry

2, 42g-sized, pots of Gentleman's Relish, or the same amount of one of the other variations – see above

20-30g grated parmesan cheese

1 beaten egg

Cooking instructions

1. Take the pastry out of fridge about 30 minutes before using. Remove the outer box. This will make the pastry easier to unroll and work with.

2. Heat the oven to 180°C

3. Unroll the pastry, leaving it on the paper it is wrapped in. Lightly roll it so it is about 30% less thick.

4. Spread the relish thinly and evenly on the pastry. Sprinkle over the parmesan cheese.

5. Roll both long edges of the pastry from the outside to meet in the middle

6. Cool in the fridge for 10 minutes

7. Slice the roll, using a sharp knife, into 6-7 mm pieces. Place on a buttered baking tray

8. Brush each piece with beaten egg

9. Slightly flatten each piece using the rolling pin

10. Sprinkle a little grated parmesan cheese on to the top of each piece

11. Cook for 15 minutes in the pre-heated oven, or until golden brown

Creative Ways to Prepare Starters and Light Lunches

Sea bass or sea bream ceviche

Ceviche originates in South America, but it is popular in many countries.
It comprises of ultra-fresh, uncooked seafood marinated in citrus juices,
red chilli and garlic. This dish reminds me of a holiday in Crete where this was
served on a warm evening in a lovely restaurant by the Mediterranean Sea.
Hopefully, this recipe captures the freshness of the fish and the zingy flavours.

Serves 2 using 120–150ml ramekins

Ingredients

1 very fresh sea bass / sea bream, filleted and skinned

Juice of 1 ½ limes and ½ lemon

Zest of 1 lime

1 large garlic clove, very finely sliced

1 red chilli deseeded and finely chopped – decrease this to ½ chilli if you like a milder taste!

3 young spring onions, finely chopped (white part only)

3–4 stalks of fresh basil leaves, pick off the leaves and chop

Salt and pepper

½–1 tbs olive oil to moisten (best quality available)

Coriander to garnish

Cooking instructions

1. Cut the fish fillets into ½ cm strips and then cut crossways to form small cubes. Place in a glass bowl. (*Tip: glass is better than metal which can transfer an unpleasant metallic background taste.*)

2. Squeeze the lime and lemon juice, plus the lime zest, over the fish. Add the finely chopped garlic, red chilli, spring onions and chopped basil leaves. Add seasoning. Moisten the mixture with good-quality olive oil.

3. Chill for 1 ½ hours in the fridge – the fish should appear opaque and waxy. Do not leave longer as the fish loses its firmness. Drain off any excess fluid.

4. Oil 2 x 150ml ramekins and double line with cling film, leaving plenty of overhang.

5. Fill the ramekins with the fish ceviche and use overhanging cling film to cover the top of the ramekins. Press down firmly and apply a light weight to the top for 20–30 minutes (e.g. an unopened tin of baked beans will work well).

6. Then take the ramekins out of the fridge and serve by inverting them onto the serving plate and removing the cling film. Drizzle good-quality olive oil over the ceviche and garnish with chopped coriander.

Serving suggestions and accompaniments

Serve with a side dish of guacamole: mash 1 ripe avocado with 1 tbs lime juice, 2 tbs finely chopped spring onion, 1 finely chopped garlic clove, ½ red chilli, deseeded and chopped, 1 tbs chopped tomato (with skins removed), salt and pepper. Mix and then gently blitz in a food processor. Drizzle in a little more olive oil to bind.

Crab timbale

This is one of my favourite dishes and I am yet to serve it to anyone who didn't like it.
It is quite rich, so if you are making it as a starter don't be too generous with the portion size!
It works equally well as a summer lunch main course.

Serves 4 as a starter

Ingredients

4 ramakins / timbale moulds (*tip: a 100ml size works well*)

350g white crab meat (*tip: your fishmonger should be able to supply fresh white crab meat. If not, see Store Cupboard,* **page 12,** *for suppliers. Do not use 'pasteurised' white crab meat for this dish as it lacks the necessary taste and texture. If white crab meat is unavailable, use a mix of fresh white and brown meat*)

½ red chilli, deseeded and very finely chopped – adjust the quantity according to taste

4 spring onions, finely chopped

1 large garlic clove finely chopped

3cm fresh ginger root, peeled and grated

Juice ½ lime

8–10 stalks of coriander. Pick the leaves off the stalks and chop

1 tbs good mayonnaise

1-2 tbs fish sauce

Pepper to season

2-3 slices smoked salmon

2 large tomatoes, skinned and chopped finely

1 large or 2 small ripe avocados, chopped. Add lime juice to prevent browning of the flesh

Salsa:

½ ripe mango, chopped

½ papaya, chopped

6 sprigs coriander. Remove the leaves from the stalks and chop

A squeeze of lime juice. Try to avoid making the salsa too wet

Cooking instructions

1. Mix the crab meat, red chilli, spring onion, garlic, grated fresh ginger, lime juice, coriander, mayonnaise, fish sauce and pepper. Do in stages as the mixture must be quite stiff to hold its shape. Adjust the flavour. (*Tip: if the lime flavour is too prominent, add 1 tsp of sweet, hot chilli sauce; if the taste needs heightening, add a dash of Worcestershire sauce or a little more fish sauce.*)

2. Oil the inside of the ramakins / timbales and line with double thickness of cling film. Cut circles of smoked salmon to fit the base of the lined timbale.

3. Add the crab meat mix to fill ⅔ of the timbale.

4. Add a layer of chopped tomato. (*Tip: remove the skins by dropping the tomatoes in boiling water for 1–2 minutes – the skin will peel off.*) Cut in half, remove the seeds and then chop.

5. Press down firmly.

6. Cover the timbales with cling film and put in the fridge overnight. (*Tip: a light weight on top helps.*)

7. About 2–3 hours from use: dice the avocado. Coat with lime juice to prevent browning. Add a little mayonnaise to bind. Season.

Recipe continued on next page.

8. Open each timbale and add a layer of avocado. Reseal timbale and replace the weight. Chill.

9. Salsa: chop ½ ripe mango and ½ papaya. Add chopped coriander and a little lime juice. Season.

Serving suggestions and accompaniments

About 30 minutes ahead of serving, take the timbales out of the fridge. To serve, invert the timbale on the serving dish and shake firmly – the timbale should come away from the mould. Remove the cling film and plate with a garnish of chopped coriander. If serving in the summer an edible flower such as a viola is a pretty addition.

Minted pea panna cotta with smoked salmon

This is quite a fiddly dish to make, but for a special occasion it is worth it. It requires the use of gelatine, but don't be put off – just follow the instructions on the packet carefully and know how much fluid you will need to set, so you can calculate the right amount of gelatine to use. I always buy the Dr Oetker brand which is widely available as gelatine leaves or powder sachets – the instructions are fail safe!

Serves 6

Recipe continued on next page.

Ingredients

6 x 75–100ml ramekins

5 medium-sized spring onions, chopped

1 garlic clove, chopped

20g butter

450g frozen petit pois – always buy best quality to get a delicate flavour

4 sprigs mint

400ml good-quality chicken or fish stock

50g grated hard goats cheese – optional

225ml double cream

Salt and pepper

½ tsp caster sugar

3 ½ leaves of gelatine – but check your final fluid quantity before making your gelatine solution

Garnish:

6 rolls of smoked salmon

4 tbs pomegranate seeds

6 sprigs pea shoots

Cooking instructions

1. Lightly oil 6 ramekins (75–100ml). (*Tip: it's best to use sunflower oil rather than butter to grease the ramekins. Butter tends to set too hard in the fridge and doesn't facilitate the release of the panna cotta when serving.*) Line the ramekins with a double layer of cling film – have enough overhanging to wrap over the top of the ramekin. This lining needs to be as smooth as possible, so the surface of the panna cotta looks smooth and professional when it is turned out.

2. Sweat the finely chopped spring onions and garlic in butter until soft. Add the petit pois and coat them in the butter. Add the mint sprigs and the stock and slowly bring to the boil. Simmer gently for 5 minutes, until the peas are soft, and then cool and drain. Keep back about 3 tbs petit pois for garnish. Liquidise the pea mix in a food processor. (*Tip: for added depth of flavour add 50g grated hard goats cheese and let it melt into the warm pea mix.*) Add the double cream. Pass through a fine sieve. Season with salt and pepper. To bring out the pea flavour add ½ tsp caster sugar.

3. Check the volume of your pea puree and make up enough gelatine to set that volume of fluid. (*Tip: the instructions are clearly described on the Dr Oetker brand – 4 leaves of gelatine set 1 pint [570ml] of fluid – so use a proportionate amount.*) Add the gelatine mix to the pea cream and mix thoroughly. Pour into the ramekins and wrap the cling film over the top. Chill overnight.

4. Bring out of the fridge about 45 minutes ahead of use (panna cotta should be set but slightly wobbly when served). Peel back the cling film on the tops of the ramekins and then invert onto the serving dishes and remove the rest of the cling film.

5. Serve with one (or more) roll(s) of smoked salmon. Garnish with cooked petit pois, a sprinkle of red pomegranate seeds for colour and pea shoots coated with a good French dressing.

Salmon and asparagus terrine

This was inspired by a Mary Berry recipe. It looks very impressive but is quite easy to make and can be made ahead of time. It can be served as a starter or as a main course for lunch. The quality of the smoked salmon is important, and it needs to be firm and not too salty.

These quantities are for a 1lb (450g) baking loaf tin

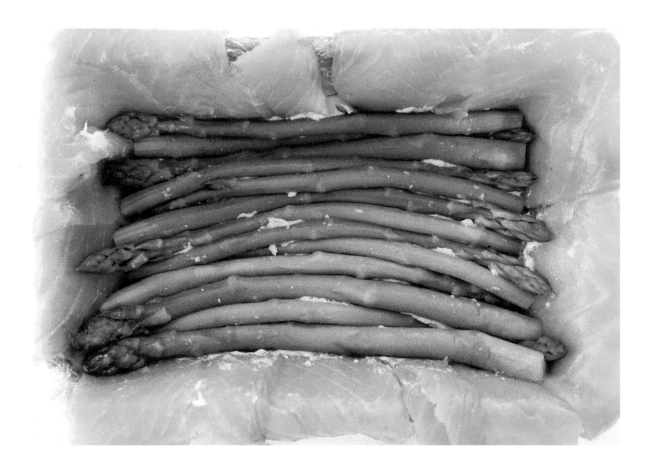

Recipe continued on next page.

Ingredients

300g fresh salmon fillet

1 tsp lemon juice

Salt and pepper

3 sprigs dill, chopped

1 tbs sunflower oil

10 long stems of asparagus – select young, evenly
  sized stems

350g smoked salmon – this needs to be cut
  longitudinally – see Store Cupboard, **page 12**,
  for suppliers

75g butter

150g full-fat Philadelphia cream cheese

2 spring onions, chopped

2 sprigs dill, chopped

3 tbs lemon juice

Garnish:

Pea shoots dipped in a French dressing

Cooking instructions

1. Cook the fresh salmon. Firstly, marinate for 15 minutes in 1 tbs lemon juice and season with salt and pepper. Dry the fillet on a paper towel. Butter one side of a sheet of baking foil and lay the salmon on this. Scatter on 3 dill sprigs and dot surface of fillet with butter. Make a foil parcel around the salmon. Place on a baking dish and cook in the oven for 15 minutes at 200°C. If using a cooking thermometer, the fillet will be done at 50°C, core temperature. If you do not have a cooking thermometer, the fish should be pink and opaque except for the deep core of the fish which should be slightly translucent.

2. Next, prepare the asparagus. Cut to fit the inside length of the loaf tin. Boil for 3–4 minutes. Drain and rinse in cold water to preserve the green colour. Cool on a paper towel.

3. Oil a 1 lb loaf tin and double line with cling film – leave sufficient overhang so the ends can be wrapped across the top of the loaf tin. (*Tip: it is better to use sunflower oil rather than butter to grease the inside of the tin – it tends to make the turning out easier.*)

4. Line the tin with the smoked salmon. Start by laying the salmon strips across the long sides of the tin, leaving plenty overhanging the sides. Then line the short sides with the salmon – again leaving an overhang – see photograph above. Leave a strip of salmon available to finish off the top.

5. Place the leftover smoked salmon and the fresh cooked salmon (skin removed) in a food processor. Add the butter, cream cheese, spring onions, dill and lemon juice. Blend thoroughly, but don't overdo it. Season.

6. Spread half the fresh salmon mix on the bottom half of the lined loaf tin. Then add the asparagus – pack the stems closely, alternating the top and bottom, so there will be a green layer when the terrine is cut open and served (see photo above). Next, add the remaining fresh salmon cream. Flap over the overhanging smoked salmon to cover the top of the terrine. Bring over the edges of the cling film to cover the terrine and press down firmly. Add the final strip of smoked salmon to close the terrine. Place in fridge with a light weight on top.

7. Serve in slices with garnish of pea shoots, lightly coated in a French dressing. Add an edible fresh flower for colour (e.g. pansy). This dish looks attractive when cut with the layer of asparagus running through the middle of the slice.

Hot smoked salmon and ricotta cheesecake on an oatcake base

This savoury cheesecake is a novelty starter or a main lunch course. I first came across it when watching a travel program about the Isle of Skye. The owner of a smokehouse in Tarskavaig enthused about this dish made with their home-smoked salmon – so I gave it a try!

Serves 8 as a starter or 6 as a light lunch

Ingredients

Base:

200g rough milled oatcake biscuits, roughly broken up

60g butter, softened

40g parmesan cheese

Black pepper

Filling:

300g fresh salmon fillet

Salt and pepper

2–3 lemon slices

6 sprigs dill, set aside 3 sprigs and then remove the
  stalks from the rest and chop

250g hot smoked salmon

2 spring onions, chopped

250g full-fat Philadelphia cream cheese

300g ricotta cheese

250ml double cream

½ tsp horseradish cream

3 eggs, beaten

Juice and zest of ½ lemon

Red pepper and cucumber sliced for garnish

Cooking instructions

1. Place the broken oatcake biscuits, the softened butter, parmesan cheese and the pepper into a food processor and blitz quickly – do not make the crumb too fine. Butter the inside of a 23cm/9-inch springform cake tin and then firmly press the oatcake mix into the bottom and sides of the tin. Chill for 20 minutes and then bake for 10 minutes at 180°C in the oven. Leave the base in the tin and cool.

2. To cook the fresh salmon, heat the oven to 200°C. Butter one side of a piece of foil and place the salmon fillet skin side down on it. Season with salt and pepper and place a couple of lemon slices and half the chopped dill on top. Fold the foil into a parcel and place on a baking tray. Cook for 8–10 minutes in the oven until the fish is just cooked (about 40°C, if using a cooking thermometer). When cooked, open the foil parcel and leave to cool.

3. When the baked salmon is cool, make the filling. Flake the hot smoked and the fresh salmon into a bowl. Add the finely chopped spring onions and the rest of the dill. Now mix in the cream cheese, the ricotta cheese and the double cream, together with the horseradish cream and 3 beaten eggs. Add the juice and zest of ½ lemon and season. Pour the cheesecake filling into the cooled oatcake base.

4. Cook for 30 minutes at 180°C. Check progress – if the filling is not quite set, but is getting brown on top, reduce the oven to 160°C and cook for a further 10 minutes. Turn the oven off and let the cheesecake cool in the oven. When done, remove and wrap in cling film and place in the fridge overnight.

5. Garnish with sliced red pepper and cucumber slices before serving.

Tempura fried squid rings with red chilli and spring onions

This is a very popular dish in pubs and restaurants, and here is how you can cook it at home. Ideally you require a deep fat fryer to cook the squid, but I will tell you how to achieve the dish if you don't have one.

Serves 4 as a starter and 2 as a main course

Ingredients

Aioli sauce:

3-4 tbs good mayonnaise

1 garlic clove (smoked is best), finely chopped

1 tbs lemon juice

Squid:

300g prepared squid (source small squid as young as possible) or deep-frozen squid rings.

Salt and pepper

½ tsp roasted chilli seeds

1 tbs plain flour

½ red chilli, deseeded, finely chopped (add more if you like a hot chilli taste!)

3 spring onions, finely sliced on the diagonal

Packet of Tempura batter mix – see Store Cupboard, **page 12**, for suppliers

Bottle of chilled sparkling water

500ml cooking oil

Lemon wedge for each person

Cooking instructions

1. Start by making a very quick aioli sauce: blitz together all the ingredients and place in the fridge until needed.

2. Take the squid out of the fridge and allow to come to room temperature, as this will reduce the cooking time. Then take the prepared squid and turn the body inside out and lightly score the inside with a sharp knife. Cut into 0.5cm thick rings. Cut each of the long tentacles into 2–3 sections. Dry the squid carefully between 2 sheets of paper towel. Season with salt, pepper and roasted red chilli seeds and then lightly dust with plain flour.

3. Make the tempura batter. I use a packeted ready-mix and make it up as described on the pack. (*Tip: using very cold sparkling water makes the batter lighter.*)

4. Prewarm oven to 100°C. Heat the oil in your deep fryer or in a heavy-based frying pan to 180°C. Dip the squid rings into the tempura batter, shake off the excess and drop into the hot oil. Cook in small batches for best results and separate the rings as they cook. When golden take the squid out of the oil and drain on a paper towel. Keep warm in the oven while cooking the remaining squid.

5. Plate onto individual dishes, scatter over the chopped red chilli and the spring onions. Serve with a wedge of lemon and pass round the aioli dipping sauce.

Serving suggestions and accompaniments (ingredients not listed above)

Serve with accompanying salad of 1 cucumber (peeled, deseeded and sliced), 50g bean sprouts, 25g watercress and add a dressing of juice ½ lime, 1 tsp fish sauce, 1 tsp red chilli finely chopped, 1 spring onion cut on the diagonal, ½ garlic clove finely chopped, small handful of coriander coarsely chopped.

Dishes Bursting with Flavour: Main Courses

Sea Bass

Sea bass is a very popular fish. It has juicy, firm, white flesh, which is very versatile and can be pan-fried, grilled, steamed, baked or barbecued whole. I prefer to cook bass as fillets as they are quick and easy to prepare. The texture and taste mean that sea bass can be flavoured in many ways. One good-sized fish prepared as fillets is sufficient for 2 people. Wild sea bass when available is a real treat!

Grilled sea bass as the perfect fast supper dish

This is a versatile fish, and the flavour can be enhanced in several simple ways, making it an excellent quick supper dish. Here are 3 ideas using flavour boosters such as basil or truffle pestos and artichoke puree. There are lots of other similar pestos sold, so try exploring those too as it is an instant way to enhance the flavour of fish!

Cooking instructions

1. Before you get started, take the fish out of the fridge and while it's coming up to room temperature (at least 15 mins), marinate the fillets in the juice of ½ a lemon for about 15 minutes ahead of cooking. Season both sides of the fish with salt and pepper. (*Tip: this minimises the cooking time and the simple lemon marinade brings out the flavours of the fish.*)

2. Dry the fish fillets on paper towel, and then brush on one of the following, easily sourced, bottled pestos and purees/creams to the flesh side of the fillet (see the section titled Store Cupboard, **page 12**, for details of where to obtain these items). This adds a much greater depth to the taste of your dish. Here are the cooking details:

Basil pesto:

Thinly coat the bass fillets with the basil pesto. Cook as described on next page, but just before cooking is completed, sprinkle the flesh side of the fish with chopped fresh basil and squeeze on a little more lemon juice. Place under the grill for 30 seconds to wilt the basil. Serve with sliced courgettes, cooked in olive oil, chopped garlic, plus 1–2 tsp of basil pesto stirred in.

Truffle pesto:

This is a delicious but quite powerful flavouring, so don't be over generous. Spread a thin layer of the truffle pesto on the flesh side of the fish. Then cook the fish as described on next page, but just before serving, sprinkle the fillets with chopped flat parsley and scatter on some roasted hazelnuts (these can be bought in ready-to-use packets in the baking section of supermarkets).

This recipe goes well with a simple mushroom sauce: slice button mushrooms or, if you want to kick this up a notch or two, use king oyster mushrooms or Forestier mushrooms. Fry them quickly in butter and add a splash of single cream and 1 tsp of the truffle pesto. Season.

Artichoke puree/cream:

There are several good brands of artichoke cream. Make a paste of equal quantities of the artichoke cream and bottled hollandaise sauce (Maille brand hollandaise is good for this). Brush onto the fish fillets. Cook as described on next page, but for a last-minute taste pop, shake some roasted flaked almonds (can be bought in the baking section of supermarkets) over the fillets and return to the grill for 30 seconds.

Serve with some sliced artichokes bottled in oil. Fry ½ garlic clove, stir in the sliced artichoke. Heat until just warm, add a squeeze of lemon juice and serve on the side.

Recipe continued on next page.

Cooking the fish fillets – this applies to all the above dishes

1. Remove the grill pan from the oven and preheat the grill to 200°C.

2. Line the grill rack with tinfoil and brush with olive oil. Lay the fish fillets, prepared as above, on the foil, skin side down. Drizzle 1-2 tbs of olive oil over the dressed fish – or add a few small knobs of butter. Cook for 4 minutes, then carefully turn the fillets over and cook for 2 further minutes. Turn the fish over again and dress it with herbs or nuts etc. as described above, and cook for 30 seconds. Check the fillets are cooked through (if using a cooking thermometer, the internal temperature should be 50°C). (*Tip: plate up as quickly as possible to avoid further cooking on the hot grill rack.*)

SE Asian-style steamed sea bass

I am a huge fan of fusion cooking which blends the best of Eastern and Western cooking techniques. This works particularly well for fish dishes. I was first introduced to this steamed sea bass dish by a wonderful Filipino nurse living with us to help look after my very aged father. She taught me the principles of SE Asian cuisine and I taught her how to cook a steak and kidney pudding… which my dad loved! I preferred the delicacy of the SE-Asian approach!

Serves 2

Recipe continued on next page.

Ingredients

You will need a bamboo steamer or a metal fan steamer

2 garlic cloves

4 spring onions, finely cut lengthways

½ red chilli, deseeded and finely chopped

2-inch piece of ginger root

2 tbs cooking oil

1 tsp sesame seed oil

1 tbs sesame seeds

1 tbs of Japanese soy sauce

Juice ½ lemon and ½ lime

2–3 tbs roasted peanuts – omit if anyone has a nut allergy

2 sea bass fillets, skinned, each cut lengthways along the natural longitudinal line

Handful of chopped coriander for dressing the finished dish

Salt and pepper

Cooking instructions

1. Take sea bass fillets out of fridge and bring to room temperature (at least 15 mins).

2. Finely chop the garlic, half the spring onions and red chilli. Peel and grate the fresh ginger root. Lightly roast sesame seeds in a frying pan – only takes 1–2 minutes. Tip onto a plate.

3. Add cooking oil and sesame oil to the frying pan and lightly fry the chopped garlic and ginger. Add the sesame seeds. Mix in soy (*Tip: I recommend a brand such as Kikkoman*), lemon and lime juice and the rest of the chopped spring onions. Add the chopped roasted peanuts for a crunchy texture. Cook the paste for a further minute.

4. Season the 2 skinned bass fillets with salt and pepper and spread the mixture on the surface of the fillets. Then roll up the fillets and secure with thin string.

5. Line the bamboo/fan steamer with foil, place the fish rolls into this. Steam for 8–10 minutes. (*Tip: if you use a food thermometer, the interior temperature of the roll should be 50°C when cooked.*) Remove the string from around the fish rolls. Sprinkle the fish with chopped coriander before serving.

Serving suggestions and accompaniments

Serve with jasmine rice and pak choi cooked with garlic and soy sauce.

Sea bass Goan curry

This is a fragrant curry which goes particularly well with fish. I have used gurnard and sea bass fillets, but this works well with brill or sea bream fillets.

Serves 4

Ingredients

4 fillets sea bass

4 fillets gurnard

16 fresh king prawns

Salt, pepper

2 tsp roasted chilli seeds

Juice 1 lime

240g jasmine rice

Curry sauce

3 tbs cooking oil

2 garlic cloves, finely chopped

3 shallots, finely sliced

1 green and 1 red chilli, deseeded and finely chopped
– add more chilli for a hotter curry

3 inches fresh ginger, peeled and grated

2 stems lemongrass, sliced lengthways and softened
with a kitchen mallet, or use 4 tsp lemongrass
puree – (see Store Cupboard, **page 12**)

3 tsp ground turmeric

3 tsp ground garam masala

6 cardamon seeds

1½ tsp mustard seeds

1 star anise

3-4 kaffir lime leaves (if dried, rehydrate in warm
water for a few minutes)

2 bay leaves

1 tbs fish sauce

1 tsp tamarind paste

1 tbs sweet chilli sauce

150ml light coconut milk

4 large tomatoes, skin removed and chopped

3 sprigs fresh Thai basil, remove the leaves from the
stems. Coarsely chop

Juice 1 lime

250ml of stock (dissolve ½ fish stock cube in warm
water)

Salt and pepper

8 sprigs fresh coriander, chopped

Cooking instructions

1. Slice the fish fillets longways and then crosscut to form large chunks. Peel the prawns. Season with salt, pepper and roasted chilli seeds. Marinate the seafood for at least 15 minutes in the juice of 1 lime.

2. Cook the jasmine rice. When cooked, wash through with hot water and place in a strainer. Cover with a clean tea towel until required. See serving suggestions on next page in order to cook the rice dome in the photograph.

3. To make the curry sauce, heat the cooking oil and then fry the sliced shallots and garlic until golden. Add all the other curry sauce ingredients. Fry for 2 minutes. Pour in the coconut milk, chopped tomatoes and add the Thai basil, the juice of a lime and 50ml of the stock. Simmer for 2–3 minutes and season to taste with salt and pepper.

Recipe continued on next page.

4. Carefully remove the woody lemongrass outer stems and discard.

5. Add more fish stock until you have sufficient sauce to cook the fish.

6. Add the prawns and cook for 1 minute. Then add the fish and cook for 3–5 minutes until just done (*Tip: don't overcook the fish as it will continue to cook while you are plating up*). Adjust the seasoning.

Serving suggestions and accompaniments

Serve with jasmine rice. For a nice professional look, oil 4 deep individual ramekin dishes and spoon equal amounts of the cooked rice into each, pushing it down so it is tightly packed. Then take the serving dishes (flat-bottomed pasta bowls work well for this dish) and invert a ramekin in the centre of each. Tap and shake sharply and the rice will come out as a dome. Place the fish around the rice and then place 4 of the prawns on the top of each dish. Spoon on the remaining sauce and garnish with chopped coriander.

Sea bream

Sea bream is an excellent everyday fish choice. It has firm, white flesh and a 'nutty' taste which will take many different flavourings. It is also very reasonably priced compared with the more luxury-end fish varieties. Definitely, one of my regular go-to dishes!

Brill

Brill is a flatfish related to turbot, and it sometimes comes off second against the 'king of fish'! However, don't overlook brill – it has many of the eating characteristics of turbot with sweet, firm flesh but is quite a lot less expensive. It has a smooth brown, almost dappled skin with a white underbelly. The fish come in various sizes, so brill can be used for 2 or 4 servings. (*Tip: One smaller fish will provide 2 good sized fillets and a medium-sized fish will provide 4 nice large fillets.*)

Cod

Cod is a large, saltwater fish with white flesh and a mild flavour, which makes it very versatile (except for grilling as it tends to fall apart). The flesh forms large flakes when perfectly cooked.

Sea bream with chorizo

Here is a dish which I think is particularly well suited to sea bream as its firm, nutty flesh is excellent with the stronger flavours of chorizo. (If you don't eat meat, then I suggest you substitute Linda McCartney's Vegetarian Chorizo and Red Pepper Sausages or Plantlife Spanish Style No Chorizo – available at supermarkets).

Serves 2

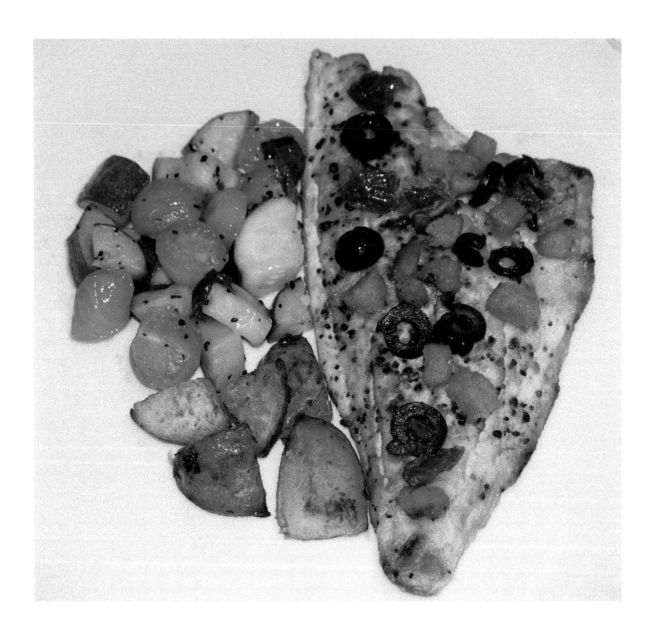

Ingredients

1 large sea bream prepared as 2 fillets

Juice of ½ lemon

Salt and pepper

½ tsp roasted chilli seeds

1 garlic clove, finely chopped

2-inch piece of chorizo sausage (or vegetarian substitute – see above), chopped into small cubes (approx. 25g)

4 large sun-dried tomatoes in olive oil, roughly chopped

8 black olives, stones removed and chopped into largish pieces

2 tsp basil pesto sauce

6 large basil leaves, chopped

Cooking instructions

1. Marinate the fish fillets in juice of ½ lemon for at least 15 minutes and let the fish come to room temperature. Season with salt, pepper and sprinkle with roasted chilli seeds.

2. Heat the grill to 210°C. Remove the grill pan beforehand and line with tinfoil and drizzle with olive oil to prevent the fish sticking.

3. Make the topping for the fish: in a frying pan quickly fry the garlic and the chopped chorizo / substitute; then add the chopped sun-dried tomatoes and black olives. Cook quickly and then drain and place on paper towel.

4. Brush each fish fillet with 1 tsp of basil pesto sauce.

5. Grill the fish for 3 minutes skin side down and then turn over and cook the other side for 3 minutes (the exact time depends on the size of the fish and the heat generated by your grill).

Serving suggestions and accompaniments

Plate the sea bream fillet and top with the chorizo / substitute, sun-dried tomato and olive mix. Decorate with chopped basil leaves.

Accompany with corn on the cob served with butter and diced courgette fried in olive oil and garlic with basil pesto added at the end. (*Tip: if you find that you made too much of the chorizo / substitute and tomato mix, then add to the courgettes!*).

Brill roasted whole on the bone

This recipe was kindly provided by Andrew Johnson, whose company has supplied the fish for these recipes. I'm sure this tasted every bit as good as it looks in the photograph!

Serves 4

Ingredients

1.5–2kg brill, whole. Scaled and fins trimmed

Juice of 1 lemon

1 lemon in thick slices

Salt and pepper

6 medium-sized waxy potatoes

4 sprigs fresh lemon thyme, leaves removed from stalks

4 sprigs fresh oregano, leaves removed from stalks

6 sprigs fresh parsley, leaves removed from stalks

20g butter

1 red pepper, deseeded and sliced

8 small ripe cherry tomatoes

2 garlic cloves, finely chopped

2 tbs extra virgin olive oil

½ cup water

8 large black olives, stones removed

3–4 sprigs fresh basil, roughly chopped

Cooking instructions

1. Take the fish out of the fridge at least 30 minutes before use. Squeeze the juice of a whole lemon over the fish and season with salt and black pepper (*Tip: season the body cavity*). Dry carefully on paper towel before cooking. Cut 1 lemon into thick slices and place in the cavity of the fish.

2. Parboil the potatoes. Cool and slice thickly.

3. Preheat the oven to 200°C.

4. Lightly score the surface of the fish on both sides. Rub olive oil all over the fish.

5. Generously butter a baking dish. Chop the fresh lemon thyme, oregano and parsley and place half on the bottom of the dish. Place the fish on top of the herbs and then sprinkle the remaining herbs on top of the fish. Cut the butter into knobs and dot on the surface of the fish.

6. Place the sliced red pepper, cherry tomatoes and the thickly sliced parboiled potatoes around the fish and sprinkle on the finely chopped garlic. Season with salt and pepper and drizzle with olive oil. Roast for 20 minutes – the core temperature of the fish will be 50°C when cooked. Just before the fish is cooked, garnish with chopped fresh basil and halved black olives. Return to the oven for 1 minute to wilt the basil.

7. Serve together with the sliced potatoes, red pepper, cherry tomatoes and olives.

Pan-fried brill with oyster mushrooms

Brill can take a quite robust cooking method and this version incorporates some autumn seasonal notes through use of mushrooms and chestnuts.

Serves 2

Ingredients

1 medium-sized brill prepared as 2 individual fillets

Juice of ½ lemon

Salt, pepper

½ tsp roasted chilli seeds

1 tbs plain flour

300ml fish stock – either made from the bones of the fish or from a fish cube / stock pot in hot water (*tip: this is a robust dish, and you could use chicken stock*)

15g butter

1 shallot, finely chopped

1 small leek, finely chopped

1 stem celery, finely chopped

2 fresh or dried sage leaves

4 stalks parsley, pick the leaves from the stalks

3 stalks thyme, remove the leaves from the stalks

20g pancetta, cubed

½ tsp roasted smoked garlic puree (to source see Store Cupboard, **page 12**)

½ tsp truffle pesto (to source see Store Cupboard, **page 12**)

2 tbs white wine (or substitute a mix of fish stock, lime zest, cranberry sauce)

15g sliced chestnuts (use a vacuum-packed brand)

2 large oyster mushrooms, coarsely sliced

1 tbs grated parmesan cheese

1–2 tbs single cream

Leaves from 2–3 sprigs of tarragon for garnish

Cooking instructions

1. Take the fish from the fridge and marinate for at least 15 minutes in half of the lemon juice, salt and pepper and ½ tsp roasted chilli seeds. Dry on paper towel. Dust with plain flour before pan-frying.

2. Make 300ml fish or chicken stock and then reduce by a half to concentrate the flavours.

3. Melt the butter and fry the finely chopped shallots, leek, celery, sage, parsley, thyme and pancetta until just turning colour. Add the reduced stock and cook for 3–4 minutes. Then add the smoked garlic puree, the truffle pesto and the white wine / substitute. Finally, add the sliced chestnuts and the mushrooms. Add the rest of the lemon juice, the parmesan cheese and the single cream. Cook for 2– 3 minutes. Adjust seasoning.

4. Pan-fry the brill fillets in sizzling cooking oil. 2 minutes on either side should be sufficient. Garnish with frsh tarragon leaves.

Serving suggestions

Sauté fresh spinach in a little butter. Drain and spread a layer about the size of each fillet on the plates. Place the brill fillet on this and finish as described above.

Cod and salmon clam chowder

Boston clam chowder is a creamy fish soup which makes a hearty main supper dish. It is popular in North America and restaurants and families have their own take on it. This is my version for you to try and then adapt to your own taste!

Serves 4

Ingredients

30 live clams

350g cod fillet, skinned and cut into large cubes

350g salmon fillet, skinned and cut into similarly sized cubes

Juice ½ lemon

Salt and pepper

500ml of fish stock – or made with a stock cube / concentrated stock pot

30g butter

50g pancetta, diced (or substitute vegan bacon)

2 white onions, chopped

1 stick celery, chopped

1½–2 tbs plain flour

200g potato, peeled and diced

300ml full cream milk

120ml single cream

2 dried bay leaves

Small can sweetcorn, drained

1 tsp Dijon mustard

20g grated hard cheese (cheddar, gruyere or parmesan)

Handful parsley, chopped

Cooking instructions

1. Scrub the clams. Heat fish stock to boiling and drop in the clams. Cook until the shells open and then drain. Reserve the stock. Remove all but 8 clams from their shells (these are needed for decoration).

2. Cut the fish into cubes and marinate for at least 15 minutes in juice ½ lemon, salt and pepper.

3. Melt the butter and fry the diced pancetta / vegan substitute until it browns. Drain and set aside. Add the onions and celery to the frying pan, cook until soft. Then mix in the flour and cook for 1–2 minutes.

4. Place the potatoes in a large pan with the milk, cream and bay leaf. Bring to the boil and simmer gently until cooked, but still firm. Add the pancetta / vegan substitute, onions, celery, sweetcorn (see point 3) and bring to a gentle boil. (*Tip: if the stock is too thin, quickly slake some cornflour with cool fish stock and add enough to get the right consistency. If the stock is too thick, add some of the fish stock.*) The soup should lightly coat the back of a spoon.

5. Add the cubed fish and very gently simmer for 3 minutes and then turn off the heat. Add the cooked clams. Adjust seasoning and add the Dijon mustard and 20g grated hard cheese. Leave the fish to complete its cooking in the soup for 2–3 minutes. Adjust seasoning.

Serving suggestions and accompaniments

Serve in bowls decorated with chopped parsley. Minted petit pois go well with this. In the US, you would have saltine crackers with this dish (see the Store Cupboard, **page 12**, for suppliers).

Crab

Crab is very versatile – it can be prepared in many ways from a simple, British-style, traditional dressed crab in the shell, through to the US favourite of fried soft-shell crab, to Singapore chilli and other SE Asian favourites. I have picked several dishes that I particularly like to cook and eat – hopefully, you will too!

For these dishes I am mainly using freshly dressed crab in the half shell as it is readily available from fishmongers. It does tend to have a high proportion of brown meat, so sometimes it's necessary to introduce some additional fresh white crab meat – see Store Cupboard, **page 12**, for suppliers. (*Tip: please don't be tempted to buy frozen or pasteurised white crab meat – it lacks both flavour and texture.*)

SE Asian crab cakes

These are easy to make and are very tasty – this recipe is quite spicy, so if you want a gentler taste, just reduce some of the garlic, chilli and Thai basil. (*Tip: I suggest that you do this in a proportionate way, so the balance of the flavours is maintained.*)

Serves 3–4

Ingredients

1 freshly dressed crab in the shell

4 spring onions, chopped

1 large garlic clove, chopped finely

1 red chilli, deseeded and chopped finely

2–3 inches fresh ginger, peeled and grated

Handful of chopped coriander

4 sprigs of Thai basil, take the leaves off the stalks

Juice and zest of 1 lime

225g cold mashed potatoes

2 tsp fish sauce

Salt and pepper

2–3 tbs unsweetened desiccated coconut

Plain flour

Cooking oil for pan-frying

3 tsp sweet chilli sauce (see Store Cupboard, **page 12**)

Cooking instructions

1. Place all the ingredients (keep back some coriander leaves for garnish), except the desiccated coconut and the plain flour, into a bowl and mix well.

2. Bring the mix to a medium-firm consistency by adding desiccated coconut which will absorb excess fluid while adding a nice depth of flavour.

3. Place mix in the fridge for about 1–2 hours for the flavours to develop.

4. Divide the mix into the number of fishcakes required and, when made, dust with plain flour. Heat oven to 180°C.

5. Heat the cooking oil in a heavy-bottomed, non-stick frying pan which is ovenproof. When sizzling, place the crab cakes in the pan – cook for 2–3 minutes each side until the outside is golden brown.

6. Place the whole frying pan into the oven (check it can withstand high temperatures) and cook for a further 3–5 minutes – until the crab cakes are hot in the middle. (*Tip: I recommend using a cooking thermometer to check that the core temperature is between 48–50°C.*) This technique avoids over frying and charring the outside of the crab cakes. Always use oven gloves to take the hot pan from the oven.

Serving suggestions and accompaniments

Serve some sweet chilli sauce on the side for drizzling over the top of crab cakes and finish with chopped coriander. Serve with stir-fried vegetables. Boiled corn of the cob and pak choi goes well with this dish, too. Or, try SE Asian-style salad (ingredients not listed above): cooked rice noodles, grated ginger, finely chopped red chilli and garlic, finely sliced sweet red pepper, spring onions, bean sprouts, a handful of chopped roasted peanuts, diced cucumber (deseeded and dried) or sliced water chestnut, coriander and mint. Make a dressing of 3 tbs lime juice, ½ tsp palm cane sugar or honey, 2 tbs sesame seed oil, 1 tsp fish sauce, seasoning. Whisk and mix into the salad.

Crab and asparagus risotto

This is my partner's signature dish – a delicious fusion of an Italian dish with fresh SE Asia flavours and spices. It needs quite a lot of careful attention during cooking, but it's worth the time and effort!

Serves 2

Ingredients

8–10 asparagus spears, woody ends removed

120g frozen petit pois

50g butter

220g arborio risotto rice

1 red chilli deseeded, finely chopped

2 garlic cloves, finely chopped

3 inches fresh ginger, peeled and grated

6 young spring onions, sliced

Zest 1 lemon and 1 lime

1 large shallot, finely diced

Juice ½ lemon and 1 lime

2 tbs desiccated coconut

150ml white wine (if you don't drink alcohol, use the same volume of fish stock – see below)

1 litre fish stock (made with a concentrated fish stock pot is best)

1 ready-dressed crab (about 200g)

1 tbs fish sauce

1 tbs sweet chilli sauce

Salt and pepper

4 stalks of Thai basil, leaves removed and coarsely chopped

Handful of coriander leaves, roughly chopped

150g high-quality small cold-water prawns

Cooking instructions

1. Cut the asparagus spears into 1cm pieces and parboil with the peas in boiling water for 2–3 minutes. Drain and run under cold water to stop them cooking further.

2. Melt 50g butter in a deep-sided frying pan. When melted, add the rice to the pan and thoroughly coat the grains in butter. Add chopped chilli, chopped garlic, grated ginger, sliced spring onions, zest of lemon and lime and chopped shallots. Cook until soft and just coloured. Add the lime and lemon juice, coconut, white wine (or additional fish stock) and half the fish stock. Gently stir the rice, ensuring that it doesn't stick to the pan. Keep adding the stock in small amounts until most of it is absorbed into the rice (there may be some left). Taste the rice at regular intervals and continue cooking until you achieve the consistency you like. (*Tip: I personally like the rice grains to be separate, soft on the outside and just a little firmer inside – i.e., al dente*). About 5 minutes before serving the dish, add the crab meat and stir thoroughly into the rice.

3. Adjust the flavours to your liking: add the fish sauce and sweet chilli sauce first, then the coriander and Thai basil. The salt and a little pepper should be last. Finally, add the small cold-water prawns and the cooked asparagus and peas. Quickly cook them and then serve in shallow pasta bowls.

Cooking instructions

Garnish with either a crab claw (see photo) or 2–3 cooked king prawns (number depends on size of prawns). Scatter chopped coriander leaves on top.

Singapore chilli crab

This is a dish to enjoy with friends who you know well and who will not mind getting very messy as it is best eaten with fingers! Worth it though! I first ate this in a Singaporean fish market and restaurant where you chose your (live) seafood, requested how you wanted it prepared and it arrived at your table beautifully cooked and served in minutes! Enjoy!

Serves 4

Ingredients

3 large or 4 medium-sized whole cooked crabs	2 tbs Japanese soy sauce
2 tbs cooking oil	400ml fish stock
3 garlic cloves, finely chopped	1 tbs fish sauce
3 inches peeled and grated fresh ginger	Juice 1½ limes
2 red chillies, deseeded, finely chopped	2 spring onions, sliced on the diagonal
4 medium tomatoes, skinned and chopped	Handful of chopped coriander
2 tbs tomato ketchup	3–4 sprigs of Thai basil leaves, chopped

Cooking instructions

1. Separate the claws from the body of the crab and then crack them so the sauce can permeate into the crab meat inside. Then cut the crab bodies into 2 pieces, discarding the 'dead man's fingers' (these are the crab's gills). (*Tip: if in doubt, ask your fishmonger to help prepare the crabs!*)

2. Heat the oil in a large wok and sizzle the garlic, ginger and chillies for 1 minute. Add the chopped tomatoes, ketchup, soy and fish stock and stir. Add the fish sauce and the lime juice. Cook for 2–3 minutes

3. Add the crab and stir-fry for 3–5 minutes or until the crab is hot and coated in the sauce. Add the spring onions, coriander and Thai basil and stir them in gently.

Serving suggestions and accompaniments

Serve the crab sections on a warmed serving dish and pour over the sauce. It's good to have finger bowls on the table and plenty of paper napkins at hand!

Crab gratin

This is a delicious dish which combines the freshness of crab
with a crunchy, cheesy topping… and it's quick to prepare.

Serves 2

Ingredients

2 empty crab shells or 2 gratin dishes

20g butter

1 shallot, chopped

15g plain flour

75ml single cream

75ml white wine (Sauvignon Blanc would be good
(or equivalent volume fish stock)

2 tbs flat parsley, chopped finely

1 pinch cayenne

½ tsp Worcestershire sauce

Zest ½ lemon

30g Gruyere cheese, grated

Salt and pepper

250g fresh, unpasteurised crab meat – white meat is
best, but mixed white and brown is fine

Juice ½ lemon

1 tsp English mustard

1 tbs flat parsley, chopped

Salt and pepper

For the topping:

4–5 tbs dried breadcrumbs (depends on the size of
your gratin dish)

Zest ½ lemon

40g Gruyere cheese, grated

Salt and pepper

Cooking instructions

1. Heat the oven or grill to 180°C.

2. Make the cheese sauce: melt the butter and add the chopped shallots. Cook until soft and lightly
   golden. Add the plain flour and cook for 1–2 minutes, stirring to ensure it doesn't burn. Add the
   single cream and the white wine / substitute. Whisk to form a smooth sauce which should coat
   the back of a spoon when done. (*Tip: if the sauce is too thick, quickly make up a small amount of fish
   stock from ¼ fish cube with an appropriate amount of water.*) Add 1 tbs parsley, cayenne, Worcestershire
   sauce, lemon zest and 30g grated cheese. Gently heat (do not boil) and cook for 2 minutes. Season
   with salt and pepper.

3. Generously butter the crab shells / gratin dishes.

4. Add the juice of ½ lemon, the English mustard and the rest of the chopped parsley to the crab.
   Season with a little salt and pepper. Divide the crab mix between the crab shells / gratin dishes.
   Spoon on the sauce so it is well moistened but not swamped.

5. Mix the breadcrumbs and lemon zest, season with salt and pepper and then scatter on top of the
   crab mix. Finish off with 40g grated Gruyere cheese. Place on a baking tray. Cook for 5 minutes
   and then check on progress every minute. Cook until the topping is golden brown.

John Dory

John Dory is a strange-looking, almost circular flatfish with a disproportionately large head and long fins. It has a large black spot on the side of the body which it uses to confuse its prey. John Dory is also known as St Pierre and the black mark is said to be the thumbprint of St Peter, the patron saint of fishermen.

John Dory has a delicate, but distinctive, flavour and firm flesh and is best pan-fried, or it can be used in bouillabaisse (see recipe). Take care not to overcook as it can easily go dry. A rich red wine sauce is also a good accompaniment for this rather meaty-textured fish.

John Dory with cannellini beans

This is a tasty winter dish with warm seasonal flavours.
The cannellini beans complement the slightly meaty texture of the fish.

Serves 2

Ingredients

2 fillets from a large John Dory fish

Juice of ½ lemon

Salt and pepper

A few roasted chilli seeds

For cannellini beans:

400g tin cannellini beans in water – chickpeas will also work well

1 shallot, chopped

½ stick celery, chopped

2 tbs pancetta, or vegan substitute bacon

1 garlic clove, finely chopped

2 medium-sized tomatoes, skin removed and chopped

5 sprigs parsley (remove leaves from stalks)

½ small glass white wine (if you don't drink alcohol omit this)

1 tbs plain flour

Cooking oil for pan-frying the fish

Parsley, chopped for garnish

Cooking instructions

1. Marinate the John Dory fillets in lemon juice for at least 15 minutes. Lightly season with salt, pepper and a few roasted chilli seeds.

2. Drain the cannellini beans and reserve the bean fluid.

3. Fry the chopped shallot, celery, pancetta / vegan substitute, garlic, until pancetta / substitute is golden and vegetables are soft. Add the chopped tomatoes, parsley and loosen with some of the cannellini bean fluid and the white wine (if omitting the wine, add a little more of the bean fluid).

4. Add the beans and cook for 7–8 minutes, adding more of the reserved fluid if the mix dries out.

5. Adjust seasoning. (*Tip: if more depth of taste is needed, try 1 tsp Worcestershire sauce and/or same amount of tomato ketchup.*)

6. Dry the fish fillets between 2 sheets paper towel and dust with plain flour. Heat the cooking oil in a heavy-bottomed, non-stick frying pan. Cook the fillets for 3 minutes, skin side down, and 2 minutes on the other.

Serving suggestions and accompaniments

Plate the John Dory fillet and garnish with parsley. Add a side helping of the cannellini beans.

John Dory in red wine jus

A red wine jus might seem a little strange to serve with fish, but John Dory has a firm, almost meaty, texture and quite a strong flavour which can take this sauce. If John Dory is not available, then try brill fillets instead. If you do not wish to use alcoholic red wine, this recipe might not be suitable for you as non-alcoholic wine will not make a tasty sauce.

Serves 2

Ingredients

2 fillets of John Dory (brill can be substituted)

Juice ½ lemon

Salt and pepper

40g pancetta /or vegan bacon substitute, cubed

15g butter

1 garlic clove, finely chopped

1 shallot, finely chopped

½ medium-carrot, scraped and finely chopped

2 white leaves of fennel, chopped (or use ½ celery stick)

2 bay leaves

½ tsp roasted chilli seeds

½ tsp ground coriander

2 glasses red wine (medium size)

2 glasses of chicken stock

1 tbs dried porcini mushrooms rehydrated in hot water

2 tsp butter mixed with 2 tsp plain flour

A little single cream to enrich the sauce

Cooking instructions

1. Marinate the fish fillets in the juice of ½ lemon for at least 15 minutes. Season with salt and pepper.

2. To make the red wine jus, fry the pancetta /vegan bacon in butter until brown (3–4 minutes). Drain the pancetta and place on a paper towel. Add the chopped garlic, shallot, carrot, fennel/ celery, bay leaves, the chilli seeds and the ground coriander. Cook over medium-low heat for 3–4 minutes. Add the red wine and the chicken stock. Increase the heat so the fluid is reduced by a half. Add the drained porcini mushrooms and cook for 5–6 minutes. Enrich and thicken with the butter and flour mix (you may not need all you have prepared). Add a little single cream if the sauce needs to be richer.

3. Dry the fish on kitchen paper and dust with plain flour.

4. Cook in cooking oil for 3 minutes, skin side down, and 2 minutes on the other.

Serving suggestions and accompaniments

Place the fish on a bed of crushed new potatoes flavoured with chopped parsley and spring onions. Pour over some of the jus and garnish with pancetta and chopped parsley. Serve the rest of the jus in a small jug.

John Dory en papillote

This is a fragrant dish and when the paper parcels are opened at the table the aromatic steam is mouth-watering! It's also quite a simple dish to prepare and definitely creates a buzz.

Serves 2

Ingredients

1 John Dory, filleted and skinned

Juice ½ lemon

6–8 baby potatoes (Jersey Royals are ideal as they have a rich taste and a lovely texture)

25g butter

2–3 small leeks, washed and finely sliced

Baking parchment

4–5 springs of tarragon, remove the leaves from the stalks

2 tbs white wine (omit this if you don't drink alcohol and add the same volume of fish stock)

Cooking instructions

1. Season the fish with salt and pepper and marinate in lemon juice for at least 15 minutes.

2. Heat the oven to 200°C. (*Tip: place a baking sheet in the oven so the fish is put on the hot surface – this will ensure it cooks quickly.*)

3. Boil the potatoes until almost cooked through. Strain, cool and then slice.

4. Melt most of the butter in a pan and sweat the sliced leeks so they cook in the butter. Season and drain.

5. Cut 4 sheets of baking parchment so they are larger than the fish fillets. Butter 1 side of each sheet. Lay out 2 sheets, buttered side up. On these, firstly place a layer of sliced potatoes. (*Tip: try to make this layer a similar dimension to the fish fillet so the parcels will look neat.*) Then spoon on the leeks cooked in butter. Finally, place the seasoned fish fillets on the leeks. Dot with butter and scatter on the tarragon leaves. Cover with the remaining sheets of baking parchment (buttered side in contact with the fish) and fold so you make 2 parcels which will contain the cooking juices. Just before closing, add 1 tbs of white wine / or fish stock to each parcel.

6. Place the fish parcels on the hot baking tray and cook for 6 minutes. (*Tip: it's good to check the cooking progress after 6 minutes – the fish will be opaque when cooked.*) Return to the oven if the fish needs a little more time.

7. Place the parcels on the serving plates and then ask the diners to open the parcels. (*Tip: it works best to ask guests to remove the top layer of baking parchment and then dispose of it on a separate plate so the fish is easier to access.*)

Serving suggestions and accompaniments

Parboil asparagus and finish it on a hot griddle so it gets nice horizontal charring marks. Serve with hollandaise sauce.

Bouillabaisse

Bouillabaisse is a delicious, highly flavoured fish stew which is made with several kinds of fish and shellfish. It originated in the port of Marseilles, France, where, it is said, it was made by the fishermen who cooked the bony fish that they could not sell. There are numerous recipes for this dish, some of which are complex and time-consuming. This is my version which uses fish caught off the UK coast and is moderately quick to prepare.

Serves 4

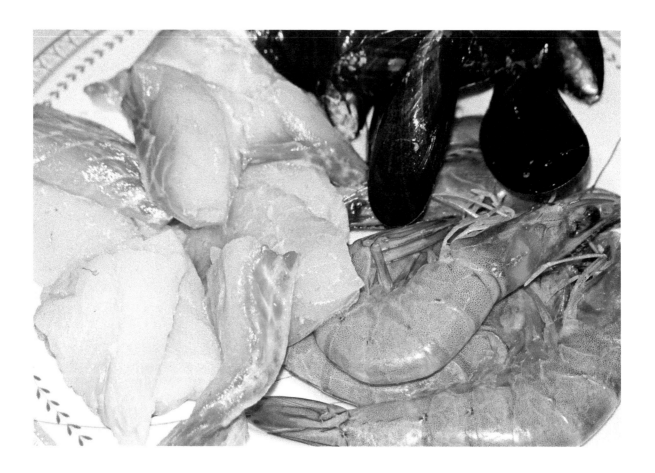

Ingredients

For the fish stock (*Tip: in this instance it is worth the time and effort to make fresh stock*):

4 tbs olive oil

1 onion, sliced

½ fennel, sliced

1 stalk celery, chopped

1 red chilli, deseeded and chopped

6 sprigs parsley

3 sprigs thyme

2 bay leaves

10 black peppercorns

1.5kg fish bones (*tip: use the ones from the fish/prawn shells listed below, plus the others that you can source from your fishmonger e.g., Dover sole, John Dory, gurnard. Also, if you can plan in advance when you will cook this dish, consider making a dish using dressed crab, shell-on prawns or, best of all, a lobster. Bag up the shells and keep them in the freezer so you can use them in the bouillabaisse broth.*)

1 litre water in which you have dissolved 1 fish stock cube or a concentrated stock pot

Cooking instructions for the fish stock

1. Using a large, heavy-based pan, heat the olive oil and fry the sliced onions, fennel, celery and red chilli until soft. Then add the fish bones and shells. Then add the parsley, thyme, bay leaves and peppercorns.

2. Pour on water with dissolved stock cube/stock pot to cover the fish bones. Bring slowly to a simmer and cook for 45 minutes. Then boil briskly to reduce the volume by about a third which will concentrate the stock – you will need about 600–700ml stock. Allow the stock to cool and then strain it – discard the bones etc.

Ingredients for the rouille:

8 tbs good-quality, olive-oil-based mayonnaise

2 cloves garlic, chopped (*tip: smoked garlic is delicious for this*)

1 tbs lemon juice

Cooking instructions for the rouille:

1. Place all the ingredients into a food processor and blitz until smooth.

2. This is handed round to guests to dollop into their bouillabaisse broth. It makes it rich and punchy.

Ingredients for the bouillabaisse:

2 John Dory skinned, prepared as 4 fillets

2 red mullets, prepared as 4 fillets

2 medium-sized gurnards skinned, prepared as 4 fillets

16 fresh prawns

24 fresh mussels in their shells

2-3 tbs olive oil

2–3 shallots, sliced

½ stalk celery, sliced

½ fennel, sliced

2 cloves garlic, chopped

1½ red chillies, chopped finely

750ml fish stock – made as above

200ml white wine. Omit this if you don't drink alcohol. Use the equivalent amount of fish stock

Bouquet garni: 3 sprigs thyme, 6 sprigs parsley,1 sprig fresh rosemary, 3 sprigs tarragon tied with string

4 large tomatoes, skinned, cored and chopped (*tip: heritage varieties will give a more authentic taste*)

Peel of 1 orange (pith removed)

2 tsp dried saffron

Salt and pepper

3 tbs olive oil, plus extra to dress the dish

Chopped parsley to garnish

Cooking instructions

1. Prepare the fish. Cut the fillets into 2–3 pieces each, shell the prawns and scrub the mussels and remove the beards.

2. Using a heavy pan (a cast-iron casserole dish or deep-frying pan are ideal), heat the olive oil and fry the shallots, celery, fennel, garlic and red chilli until soft. Add fish stock, white wine (or add equivalent amount of additional fish stock), bouquet garni, the chopped tomatoes, orange peel and dried saffron. Boil until reduced by approximately a quarter. Remove the bouquet garni. Taste and season with salt and pepper. (*Tip: if you want to increase the depth of flavour at this point, add 1 tbs tomato puree and ½–1 tsp paprika.*) Strain the stock. You require 700ml stock.

3. Heat the broth until simmering, add the fish, prawns and the mussels – cook for 5 minutes or until the fish is cooked, the prawns are pink and the mussel shells are open and mussels are lightly cooked. Adjust seasoning of the broth.

4. To dish up, use flat-based bowls – pasta dishes work well. Place equal portions of the fish in each dish, then add 4 prawns and 6 mussels per dish. Pour the fish broth over the seafood. Garnish with chopped parsley.

Serving suggestions and accompaniments

Hand round the rouille and ask each person to drop 1–2 tbs into the broth and then gently stir it in. Hand round sliced warm baguette. Oven chips are a tasty accompaniment – and a green salad with a tangy French vinaigrette dressing.

Hake

Hake is a large, deep-sea fish and a member of the cod family. It has firm white flesh and is a cost-effective choice compared with cod/halibut etc. It can be cut into fillets or steaks. It can also take some strong accompanying flavours. It is much loved by the Spanish, so I have added a suitable recipe!

Oven-baked hake with spinach and chorizo

I first had this dish in Spain – the Spanish love meluza. This recipe uses some nice paprika and chorizo flavours which give it an authentic taste.

Serves 2

Ingredients

2 x 250g hake fillets

Juice ½ lemon

Salt and pepper

1 tsp roasted chilli seeds

2 tsp basil pesto

1 tsp smoked paprika

250g bag of spinach leaves

4 smallish new potatoes, parboiled and thickly sliced

30g chorizo sausage, chopped. Alternatively, substitute Linda McCartney's vegetarian Chorizo and Red Pepper Sausages or Plantlife Spanish-style No Chorizo

6 large sun-dried tomatoes in oil

1 garlic clove, finely chopped

10 good-quality black olives, stones removed

Cooking instructions

1. Marinate the hake for at least 15 minutes in juice of ½ lemon, salt and pepper and roasted chilli seeds. Pat dry with paper towel when finished. Brush surface with basil pesto.

2. Lightly dust hake fillets with the smoked paprika.

3. Wilt the spinach and extract as much of the cooking fluid as possible. Parboil the potatoes and slice.

4. Fry the chorizo / substitute and combine with the spinach, reserving some for garnish. Heat oven to 200°C.

5. Assemble in a buttered dish. The first layer is the parboiled potatoes and chopped sun-dried tomatoes (*tip: drizzle some of the olive oil from the bottled tomatoes over the potatoes*), then add a layer of spinach, finely chopped garlic and chorizo / substitute, place the hake on top. Dot with butter.

6. Loosely cover with tinfoil and cook for 10–12 minutes in a hot oven (200°C). Remove the foil, scatter chopped black olives on the hake. Cook until done – the fish flakes should separate when gently prised apart. If using a cooking thermometer, the core temperature should be 50°C.

Serving suggestions and accompaniments (ingredients not listed above)

This would go well with a baked, stuffed tomato or red pepper using breadcrumbs, sun-dried tomatoes, thyme, oregano, parsley, garlic, paprika, black olives, any leftover chorizo / substitute sausage.

Halibut

Halibut is one of my favourite fishes – it is a large, saltwater flatfish with beautiful white flesh that has an almost gleaming appearance when it's really fresh. It can be cut into steaks (which are across the body of the fish and include the central bones) or fillets (which are cut along the length of the fish and do not have bones).

Take care in cooking halibut – it is very easy to overcook, and the proteins in the flesh denature, causing it to become unpleasantly fibrous and dry, and it loses its flaky texture

Pan-fried halibut – or posh fish and chips!

I prefer halibut cut as steaks about 2½cm thick. If it's a good-sized fish,
one steak can be cut into two portions of about 200g each.

Serves 2

Ingredients

2 x 200g halibut steaks (*tip: don't cut the steaks too thick. They will take longer to cook and it's easy to overcook this fish*)

Juice ½ lemon

Salt and pepper

A few roasted chilli seeds

2 tbs plain flour

Cooking oil for pan-frying

Wilted spinach

Melted butter as garnish

Chopped roasted pistachios or hazelnuts for garnish

Cooking instructions

1. Take the halibut out of the fridge well ahead of use to allow it to come to room temperature (reduces the cooking time). At least 15 minutes before cooking, marinate the fish in lemon juice and season with salt and pepper. Sprinkle the surface with a few roasted chilli seeds.

2. Carefully dry the halibut steaks between sheets of absorbent paper towel. Place the flour on a plate and dip the steaks into it to lightly cover all surfaces.

3. Heat the oven to 200°C – this is to finish off the fish if the surface becomes too brown when pan-frying.

4. Heat the cooking oil in a non-stick, heavy-based, ovenproof frying pan. Once sizzling, fry the halibut on both sides until golden brown and the flakes can be gently prised apart (this will be 3 minutes on each side according to the thickness of the steak). If you have a cooking thermometer, the fish should be 48–50°C at its centre (above this temperature it will become fibrous). (*Tip: if the fish is turning too brown, and is not fully cooked, place the whole frying pan in the oven at 200°C. Check it can withstand the high temperature. Check it at half-minute intervals as it will cook fast. Be sure to use oven gloves when you take the frying pan out of the oven!*)

5. Once cooked, turn onto a plate and cover, rather than leave in the frying pan, as it will continue to cook!

6. Serve on a bed of wilted spinach and cover the fish surface with lightly roasted and chopped pistachios/hazelnuts. Pour over melted butter.

Serving suggestions and accompaniments:

Boil 150g petit pois with 2–3 mint leaves for 3 minutes. Strain and pass through a sieve to remove the outer pea shells. Mix in 1 tbs butter, ½ tbs plain flour, half a beaten egg and 2 tbs single cream. Season. Butter 2 x120ml ramekins and spoon in the pea puree. Cover with buttered tin foil and cook in a water bath in the oven for 10 minutes. When cooked, invert onto the serving plate.

Make 2 portions of oven chips (remember these often take 15–20 mins to cook so factor this into your preparation time!). Plate up as in the photo.

Halibut curry with mango

The dense flesh of halibut makes a great curry. I recommend being delicate with the curry spices, so they enhance, rather than overwhelm, the taste of the fish. Take great care not to overcook the halibut as it readily loses its texture.

Serves 2

Ingredients

300g halibut, skinned and diced into 2–3cm cubes

Juice 1 lime

½ mango, must be firm and not too ripe

3 tbs cooking oil

6 uncooked king prawns

200ml light coconut milk

Handful of coriander, chopped – use some for garnish

For curry paste:

1 medium-sized chilli, halved, deseeded and chopped

Grated zest and juice of 1 lime

2 tsp lemongrass puree (for supplier, see Store Cupboard, **page 12**) or 2 stems of fresh lemongrass. Tenderise them with a kitchen mallet to release their flavour

2–3-inch piece ginger root, peeled and chopped

2 garlic cloves, chopped

1 shallot, chopped

5 leaves of Thai basil – take the leaves off the stalks

1 tbs fish sauce

Cooking instructions

1. Marinate the cubed halibut in juice of ½ lime for at least 15 minutes

2. Prepare the mango. Peel and cut into 1-2cm cubes and pour over the juice of ¼ lime

3. To make the curry paste: put all the curry ingredients into a food processor and blitz into a course paste. Place 1 tbs oil in a heavy-bottomed frying pan and cook the paste for 1 minute.

4. Heat 2 tbs oil in another heavy-bottomed frying pan and, when hot, add the halibut cubes and the peeled prawns and sear them quickly. Add the fried curry paste and coconut milk – bring up to a simmer and cook for 3 minutes. Add the chopped mango and cook for a further minute. Add more coconut milk if required.

5. Check seasoning – for an authentic taste, add fish sauce rather than salt. (*Tip: adding more of the lime juice will sharpen the flavours.*) Add chopped coriander just before serving, keeping back sufficient for garnish.

Serving suggestions and accompaniments

Serve with jasmine rice, with some desiccated coconut, quickly browned in a frying pan, folded through it. (*Tip: for a professional finish, oil a timbale/ramakin mould for each person and fill with rice, pressing it down tightly. Invert the moulds and tap the bottom sharply and the rice will come out in a nice dome.*) Place these in a centre of open bowls (one for each person) and arrange the fish curry around it, adding extra sauce.

Poached halibut with mussels
or clams on a spinach bed

This is a delicious blend of flatfish and shellfish. This dish was inspired by a visit to a restaurant on the Isle of Gigha off the west coast of Scotland. The island was bought by the community in 2002 and the Gigha Halibut Fish Farm which supplies halibut internationally was started.

Serves 2

Ingredients

2 x 180g halibut steaks or fillets

Juice ½ lemon

Salt and pepper

300g mussels, cleaned and de-bearded. You can use the same weight of clams, if preferred

200g bag spinach

40g butter

1 shallot, finely chopped

1 garlic clove, finely chopped

200ml white wine. If you wish to avoid alcohol, then use the same volume of fish stock

50ml single cream

Handful parsley, chopped

Cooking instructions

1. Take the fish out of the fridge at least 15 minutes ahead of cooking and marinate in lemon juice for 15 minutes. Season with salt and pepper.

2. Preheat your oven to 100°C.

3. Clean the mussels and cut off the beards. (*Tip: I prefer to cut the beard rather than pull it off – I feel it is more humane.*) If using clams, scrub the shells to remove any sand.

4. Wilt the spinach in a little salted water. Strain and then add a knob of butter and cook for a further 1–2 minutes. Check seasoning. Keep warm.

5. Heat 25g butter in a heavy, non-stick frying pan. Cook the shallot and garlic for 2–3 minutes until soft. Add the white wine / or fish stock and bring to the boil. Add mussels / clams and cook at a high heat until they open (3–4 minutes). Discard any that don't open. Remove all but 6 of the mussels / clams from their shells and set aside. Strain and keep the cooking liquor. (*Tip: take care to avoid any of the gritty residue getting into the liquor.*)

6. Place the halibut steaks in the mussel / clam poaching fluid and add half the chopped parsley. Cook very gently for about 3 minutes, depending on the thickness of the fish. Then turn the fish over to poach the other side and cook for a similar time. Spoon the fluid over the fish frequently to keep it moist. (*Tip: if you are using a cooking thermometer the fish will be ready between 45–48 °C – i.e., just before it is completely cooked.*) Place the halibut on a plate, remove the outer skin and cover with foil. Place in the oven for a few minutes while you finish the dish. (*Tip: you need to work quickly on the last stage to prevent the fish overcooking.*)

7. Add the remining butter to thicken the fish liquor and to make a sauce. (*Tip: do not let the sauce boil.*) Add the single cream to make the sauce richer. Add the shellfish and warm through.

Recipe continued on next page.

Serving suggestions and accompaniments

Place a portion of the spinach on the plate and position the halibut on top. Serve the shellfish around the fish, ensuring that each plate has some of the shells containing the mussels/clams. Pour the sauce around the fish and finish with chopped parsley.

Serve with celeriac and mashed potato. (*Tip: adding ½ tsp of nutmeg brings this to life!*)

Lobster and Langoustine

Lobster is very impressive – a beautiful spectrum of blue colours when alive and scarlet red when cooked. They have two large front claws and a long muscular back section with 8 walking legs. The flesh is succulent and sweet and one of the top delicacies in the world of shellfish.

Many people will say that the *only* way to eat lobster is cold with a simple salad and buttered boiled baby potatoes (preferably Jersey Royals) and home-made mayonnaise. I definitely agree that this is a wonderful way to showcase the subtleties of flavour, but I also want to provide two tried-and-trusted lobster recipes.

Langoustines are also known as Dublin Bay prawns or scampi. They are smaller than lobsters (about 25cm) and are pinkish-brown. They are delicious and I have also added a recipe for you to try

Lobster

Langoustine

Lobster thermidor

This is a popular dish, but the sauce is often rather heavy and over-cheesy. I have created a much lighter version here, which aims to complement the natural sweetness of the lobster and to heighten its distinctive flavour.

For a main course, you will need one pre-cooked lobster per person. Ask your fishmonger to cut the lobsters in half along the length of the body and crack the claws. Take care to keep any of the juices that might run out.

Ingredients

Lobster (cooked) per person

For the stock:

Keep half the shell of each lobster plus its claw shells and its legs for stock

30g butter

1 shallot, chopped

1 stalk celery, chopped

2 white leaves of fennel, chopped

1 garlic clove, chopped

2 spring onions, chopped

1 carrot, chopped

2–3 sprigs thyme

4–5 sprigs parsley

1 star anise

2 dried bay leaves

500ml water

125ml white wine. If you do not drink alcohol, then add an additional 125ml fish stock

3 tbs double cream

80gm good quality grated gruyere cheese

½ tsp English mustard

1 tarragon sprig per lobster, remove the leaves from the stem

Salt and pepper

Cooking instructions

1. Prepare the cooked lobsters. Carefully remove the meat from the body and claws of the lobster. Dice into 1cm cubed pieces. Cover with cling film and put to one side in the fridge. Scrape out the cavity of the lobster and twist off the auxiliary legs. Keep one half of the body shell for presentation (see photo opposite), and use the empty claw shells, the legs and the other half of the body shell for stock.

2. Make the shellfish / lobster sauce. Fry the shallot in butter until golden. Then add the chopped celery, fennel, garlic, spring onions, carrot, thyme, parsley, star anise and dried bay leaves. Add the lobster shells and legs and cover with the water. If you have accumulated any prawn shells in the deep freeze, add those to the stock pot! Bring to a simmer and remove any scum that collects. Continue to simmer for 20 minutes. Strain (at least twice) and then increase the heat and reduce to ½ the volume. Add the wine / additional fish stock and the double cream, the mustard and half the gruyere cheese. Stir continuously. Season. The consistency should coat the back of a spoon. (*Tip: If the sauce needs thickening, slake 1 tbs cornflour in a little water and add to the sauce in small amounts – stirring all the time over a gentle heat. Stop once the sauce consistency is appropriate*).

3. Pack the lobster cubes back into the shells and spoon over the lobster sauce (*Tip: Do not use too much sauce – the lobster just needs to be coated*). On top, sprinkle on the remaining gruyere cheese and some chopped tarragon leaves. Bring the grill up to 200°C. Line the grill tray with foil and then place the filled lobster on the grill pan. Cook under the grill for 4–5 minutes, until the cheese on top of the lobsters has become golden brown.

Recipe continued on next page.

Serving suggestions and accompaniments

Serve with high-quality oven chips and asparagus. Hand round any additional sauce at the table. (*Tip: keep any leftover sauce and add to the ingredients for the next lobster stock – I'm sure you can tell I'm a big supporter of fresh, home-made stock!*)

Lobster curry in fragrant coconut milk

This is a memorable special-occasion meal – delicate Thai curry flavours to complement the sweetness of the lobster meat. Fun to cook and even better to eat!

Serves 2

Recipe continued on next page.

Ingredients

2 cooked lobsters

For the curry paste:

2 medium-size red chillies, deseeded, chopped. Add more or less to taste

1 shallot, chopped

2 garlic cloves, chopped

2-3 inches fresh ginger, peeled and sliced

1 large, or 2 smaller, lemongrass stalks. Soften with a kitchen mallet

1 tsp shrimp paste

3 fresh Kaffir lime leaves

½ tsp ground coriander

1 tbs cooking oil

For lobster curry:

1 tbs cooking oil

8 okra, sliced

1 pak choi, finely slice the white parts

3 inner Chinese cabbage leaves, finely slice the stalks

200ml light coconut milk

2–3 fresh Kaffir leaf

5 Thai basil sprigs, with stalks removed

Ground roasted chilli seeds

1 tbs fish sauce

¼–½ tsp tamarind paste, the strength of flavour can vary between brands

Juice ½ lime

Salt and pepper

1 tbs cooking oil

Garnish with chopped coriander leaves

Cooking instructions

1. Prepare the cooked lobsters. Crack the shells and remove the meat from the tails and the claws. (*Tip: Keep the meat intact and in large pieces.*) Pick over the legs for any additional meat. (*Tip: Freeze the shells for making stock at a later date.*) Bring the lobster meat to room temperature before cooking, thus reducing the overall cooking time.

2. Place all the curry paste ingredients in a food processor and blend until smooth. Heat a frying pan, add 1 tbs cooking oil and cook the curry paste for 2 minutes.

3. Using a deeper frying pan, heat a further 1 tbs cooking oil and, when hot, slightly soften the okra, sliced pak choi and Chinese cabbage (2 minutes). Remove from the pan, place on a plate and cover.

4. Take 3–4 tbs of the curry paste and place in the frying pan. Add the coconut milk, ground roasted chilli seeds, Kaffir leaves and the chopped Thai basil leaves. Bring slowly to a simmer. Add the fish sauce, tamarind paste and lime juice. Bring to a gentle simmer and cook for 2 minutes. Sieve the curry sauce to make a smooth liquid. To this liquid add the warm okra, pak choi and Chinese cabbage. Simmer for 1 minute, or until warmed through. (*Tip: taste the sauce – if*

too sour from the lime juice and tamarind, add ¼ tsp sugar; palm sugar is best or golden caster sugar.) Add the lobster meat to the curry sauce and cook very gently until the lobster meat is warm. *(Tip: do not overcook as the lobster meat will toughen and lose flavour.)* Add a little salt to the sauce, to suit your palate.

5. To plate: spoon about half the sliced okra, pak choi and Chinese cabbage onto 2 plates. Cut the 2 lobster tails into slices and place half on each warmed plate, laying it on the okra etc. Spoon on the curry sauce and finish with some more okra, pak choi and Chinese cabbage. Then add 2 lobster claws to each plate. Garnish with chopped coriander leaves.

Serving suggestions and accompaniments

Cook jasmine rice. Fold through toasted, unsweetened desiccated coconut. Oil two single-portion ramekins. Fill with the cooked jasmine rice. Press down. Invert the ramekin and shake firmly. Place one moulded rice portion on each plate alongside the lobster curry. *(Tip: if using this jasmine rice accompaniment, plate this before the lobster.)*

Grilled langoustines in garlic butter

This is a very simple dish to make – it relies entirely on the
freshness of the shellfish as there is a minimum of cooking.

Serves 2

Ingredients

10 fresh, uncooked langoustine

Juice 1 lemon

Salt and pepper

40g butter (allow it to come to room temperature)

2 garlic cloves, finely chopped

6 sprigs parsley, chopped

Cooking instructions

1. Place the langoustines on their backs. With a sharp knife, make an incision along the length of the body, taking care not to go right through the fish. Open the incision. Squeeze on the juice of 1 lemon and season with salt and pepper. Leave to marinate for at least 15 minutes. Dry the langoustines on a paper towel.

2. Using the back of a fork, mix the room temperature butter and garlic. Place 2–3 knobs of the garlic butter into the opening in the langoustines. Chill.

3. Remove the grill tray from the oven and heat the grill to 210°C.

4. Cut a piece of cooking foil to line the grill tray. Butter generously before placing it on the tray. Arrange the langoustines on the buttered side of the foil. Place under the grill for 2–3 minutes. Check on the progress every minute until cooked and golden. Dress with the chopped parsley.

Serving suggestions and accompaniments

Serve with wedges of lemon and plenty of napkins to mop up the buttery juices. High-quality oven chips and a green salad make good accompaniments.

Mackerel

To my eye, mackerel is a very attractive fish with striking black stripes on a green-blue iridescent back with a silver belly. It has health-giving omega-3 fish oils and is rich in vitamins A and D. It is particularly well suited for grilling, pan-frying, or barbecuing.

Mackerel with horseradish
and grapefruit segments

Serves 2

Ingredients

2 mackerel – ask the fishmonger to prepare them as butterflied or boneless fillets

Juice ½ lemon

Salt and pepper

2 tsp horseradish sauce

2 tsp ready-made, bottled hollandaise sauce (see Store Cupboard, page 12, for good brand/stockists)

1 tsp Dijon mustard

1 pink fleshed grapefruit

Cooking instructions

1. Marinate the fish for at least 15 minutes in the juice of ½ lemon and season with salt and pepper.

2. Brush the fish with a creamy paste made of the horseradish and hollandaise sauces and Dijon mustard. Allow this to permeate the fish for about 10 minutes before cooking (while you prepare the vegetables etc).

3. Peel a juicy red grapefruit, removing the outer pith. Using a sharp knife, cut between the membranes thus creating segments.

4. Remove the grill tray and heat the grill to 210°C. Line the tray with tinfoil and drizzled with olive oil. Place the fish on the tray and cook for 4 minutes on the flesh side and 2 minutes on the skin side – until light golden coloured. The flesh should be firm to the touch.

5. Decorate the fillets with the grapefruit segments.

Serving suggestions and accompaniments

A couple of quick side salads include:

A dill potato salad: cook new potatoes and, when cool, dice them. Add sliced baby gherkins and finely diced spring onion. Fold in 1–2 tbs good mayonnaise. Chill before serving. Dress with chopped dill and drizzle on some good olive oil.

A fennel and beetroot salad: very quickly parboil chopped fennel. Add sliced raw apple (squeeze some lemon juice over the apple to prevent it from going brown), spicy beetroot and dill. Moisten with a good mayonnaise. (*Tip: add the sliced spicy beetroot at the very last minute so it doesn't stain the other ingredients.*)

Mussels

Mussels have a distinctive smell when fresh – rather like salty sea air. They should not smell overly 'fishy'. The glossy black bivalve shells should be tightly closed. If you find any which are open, tap sharply with a knife and they should close – if they don't, discard them. After trying several ways to cook mussels, the classic moules marinière is hard to beat, so I kept with a very traditional approach on this one, with a SE Asia twist as an alternative!

Mussels are also excellent as a garnish in a wide range of fish dishes, providing a contrasting flavour and taste.

Moules marinière

I love mussels, especially when they are really fresh and bursting with flavour. I have an especially good memory of taking my father to Bruges in Belgium for his eightieth birthday. We walked about five or six miles round the city and then he devoured a massive serving of moules et frites sitting beside one of the canals, washed down with strong Belgian beer – the walk back was slower! I hope this recipe will be as good!

Serves 4

Ingredients

2kg live mussels (*tip: mussels can be kept for 24 hours in a bowl in the fridge; allow the air to circulate*)

2 shallots, chopped

1–2 garlic cloves, chopped

20g butter

Bouquet garni: celery stick, parsley, thyme, 2 bay leaves, tied loosely in a bunch with string

½ bottle of dry white wine (the liquor resulting from this dish is one of the best aspects, so try to use a reasonable wine). If you do not drink wine, substitute the wine with fish stock – or consider the SE Asian alternative at the foot of the page.

100ml single cream

Small handful flat parsley, chopped

Salt and pepper

Sliced fresh baguette

Cooking instructions

1. Heat the oven to 100°C.

2. Prepare the mussels: place in cold water and scrub off any sand or seaweed etc. Cut off the beards. Rinse well. Any shells that don't close should be discarded.

3. In a wide, flat frying pan, cook the shallots and the garlic in the butter, adding the bouquet garni towards the end. Add the wine / additional fish stock and bring slowly to the boil, to maximise the flavours from the herbs. Put the mussels into the wine / stock in 2 batches. Cook each batch for 3–4 minutes, until the mussels open. Discard shells that don't open. Place the first batch in the serving dish and loosely cover with foil. Put this in the pre-warmed oven (*tip: the oven is set very low to keep the mussels warm, not to cook them*) whilst you cook the second batch of mussels.

4. Cook the second batch of mussels and place them in the serving dish in the oven.

5. To make the sauce, remove the bouquet garni and add the cream. Adjust seasoning. Strain the sauce over the mussels. Garnish with the chopped parsley. Serve with plenty of fresh baguette to mop up the delicious liquor. (*Tip: if you have some of the sauce left, you could freeze it and then use it to make a mussel risotto at a later date.*)

Alternative (ingredients not listed above)

This is suitable for those who do not drink alcohol.

Thai mussels are delicious. Fry 4 spring onions, 1–2 garlic cloves, 1 red chilli – all chopped. Add 400ml light coconut milk, a squeeze of lemongrass puree, a handful of coriander, 2–3 sprigs of Thai basil with the leaves removed from the stalks, 1 tbs fish sauce and juice of 2 limes. Simmer for 5 minutes and then increase the heat and add the mussels until cooked.

Pasta

I love Italian food, and shellfish goes very well with pasta – there are lots of recipes for prawn or seafood linguine. I have chosen a couple of my personal favourite recipes, which are delicious and quick to prepare.

Tip: I would suggest you try to avoid your pasta dishes becoming too heavy. Italians like to differentiate flavours in their dishes, and sauces should complement the pasta, not overwhelm it – either in flavour or quantity!

Spinach and ricotta ravioli with crab sauce

This dish is a bit of a cheat! If you like to make your own pasta, that's terrific, but, if like me, you are always in a hurry, then a pre-made packet of good-quality ravioli filled with a generous amount of ricotta and spinach works well. Always check that the pasta isn't too thick as it will expand with cooking and could be too heavy for this dish.

Serves 2–3, depending on the size of the pasta portion!

Ingredients

1 good-sized pack of good quality pre-made ricotta and spinach ravioli

1 shallot, chopped finely

2 garlic cloves, chopped finely

½ red chilli, deseeded and chopped

2 tbs olive oil for frying

1 tbs plain flour

6–8 sprigs flat leaf parsley, remove stalks and chop coarsely

½ tbs tomato paste

1 lemon, zested

200ml fish stock (*tip: ideally, try to make this yourself from stockpiled seafood shells that you may have bagged up and put in the freezer for an occasion such as this!*)

Dressed crab in the shell

2–3 tbs single cream

15g parmesan cheese

¼ tsp Dijon mustard

2 sprigs basil, chopped coarsely

Bag of spinach

Cooking instructions

1. First make the crab sauce. Sauté the shallot, garlic, red chilli in a little olive oil until soft and golden. Add the plain flour and cook for 1 minute, stirring all the time. Stir in half the parsley, the tomato paste, the lemon zest and add the stock gradually to form a sauce which will coat the back of a spoon. Add the crab meat. Bring to a gentle simmer. Add the single cream, 2 tbs grated parmesan cheese and the Dijon mustard. If the sauce is too thin, add a little cornflour slaked in cold fish stock, but avoid making it heavy.

2. Cook the ravioli and drain – use a little of the pasta water if you need to loosen the crab sauce. Season the pasta.

3. Add the pasta to the sauce and serve in pasta bowls garnished with the rest of the chopped fresh parsley and the basil.

4. Serve wilted spinach on the side.

Spaghetti alle vongole (clams)

This is a favourite Italian shellfish dish, and I have certainly done my share of enjoying this delicious dish! Some recipes add cream… the authentic dish would not include this.

Serves 2

Ingredients

600g fresh clams in their shells

Spaghetti or linguine: a portion for 2 people

3 tbs olive oil

1 shallot, finely chopped

2 cloves of garlic, finely chopped

1 red chilli, deseeded, finely chopped

6–8 small, sweet tomatoes, chopped roughly

125ml dry white wine. (If you do not drink alcohol, then substitute with the same volume of fish stock)

Salt and pepper

Handful parsley and basil, chopped for garnish

Extra virgin olive oil

Cooking instructions

1. Clams can be kept in a bowl in the fridge for 24 hours. Make sure there is air circulating. Rinse the clams in several changes of very cold water. Discard any that are damaged.

2. Cook the pasta to your liking.

3. Heat the olive oil in a large, flat frying pan and add the shallot, garlic and the chilli. Fry for 1 minute. Stir in the chopped tomatoes, add the wine (or same volume of fish stock) and salt and pepper. Bring to the boil for 1 minute.

4. Drop the clams into the liquid and cook briskly for 3–4 minutes until the shells open and the shellfish are lightly cooked. Adjust the seasoning and add the chopped parsley.

5. Drain the pasta – add a little of the pasta cooking liquor to the clam sauce if it looks dry. Mix the pasta into the clam sauce.

6. Serve with a couple of glugs of good olive oil drizzled on top with more parsley and chopped fresh basil.

Serving suggestions and accompaniments

Napkins and finger bowls are essential!

Prawns

King prawns (also known as crevettes) are farmed and consumed in huge quantities worldwide. If possible, try to find a sustainable source which has not been farmed in warm waters, as the taste will be much improved.

Prawns have a naturally salty-sweet flavour. They are very versatile and can be cooked in numerous ways. I have chosen four dishes that are easy to make using raw king prawns/ crevettes and showcase different methods of cooking.

King prawns, butterflied, in a coconut and panko tempura batter

These crunchy prawns will fly off the dish!
Always cook a few more than you think you need!

Serves 2

Ingredients

8–10 raw large king prawns/crevettes, the number depends on their size and your appetite!

Juice ½ lemon

Salt and pepper

Roasted chilli seeds

Tempura batter mix – for suppliers see Store Cupboard, page 12

30–40g plain flour

30g panko crumbs

30g unsweetened desiccated coconut

3–4 tbs cooking oil

Recipe continued on next page.

Cooking instructions

1. Take the prawns out of the fridge and marinate them for at least 15 minutes in lemon juice and season with salt and pepper and flakes of roasted chilli seeds. Dry them carefully on a paper towel to ensure that they fry in the oil and do not boil and lose their taste and structure.

2. Prepare the prawns: cut off the legs and peel off the shells – try to keep the head and tail in place as it adds to the presentation. (*Tip: keep the discarded shells in a plastic bag in the freezer as they will make great seafood stock, as and when required!*) To butterfly the prawns: cut them along the back from head to tail, but do not cut right through the fish. Remove the black thread – this is present in wild prawns but not generally in farmed fish as they are starved prior to being processed. Flatten out the body as a butterfly.

3. Make up the tempura batter as instructed on the box (see store cupboard for suppliers, **Page 12**) – this recipe uses about 125g of the dry mix. (*Tip: using cold, sparkling water lightens the batter. Also, add a pinch of salt.*)

4. Dust the dried prawns with plain flour, then dip them into the batter, coating them evenly and draining off the excess. (*Tip: use kitchen tweezers to hold the prawns, if you have them available.*) Finally, roll the prawns into a mix of the panko crumbs and desiccated coconut, making sure they are evenly coated. If the panko is rather coarse, crush it with a rolling pin before you start.

5. Preheat the oven to 100°C.

6. Heat the cooking oil in a heavy-bottomed, non-stick frying pan. When sizzling, drop in the coated prawns – it is best to do this in small batches to ensure they are well spaced, but work quickly as the prawns cook very fast. Do not overcrowd as they will not cook sufficiently rapidly to become crispy. Cook for 1–2 minutes on either side. The speed of cooking depends on your frying pan – the prawns should be golden brown. If you have too many to cook together, place the first batch on a serving dish loosely wrapped in foil and keep warm in the preheated oven.

Serving suggestions and accompaniments

Serve with corn on the cob and a side salad.

Prawn, asparagus and pea risotto

Risotto is my partner's signature dish, and it always tastes delicious, so here are the notes I made whilst he was cooking it. This isn't a quick-fix supper dish, but the extra effort it takes is definitely worth it!

Serves 2–3, depending on appetite size

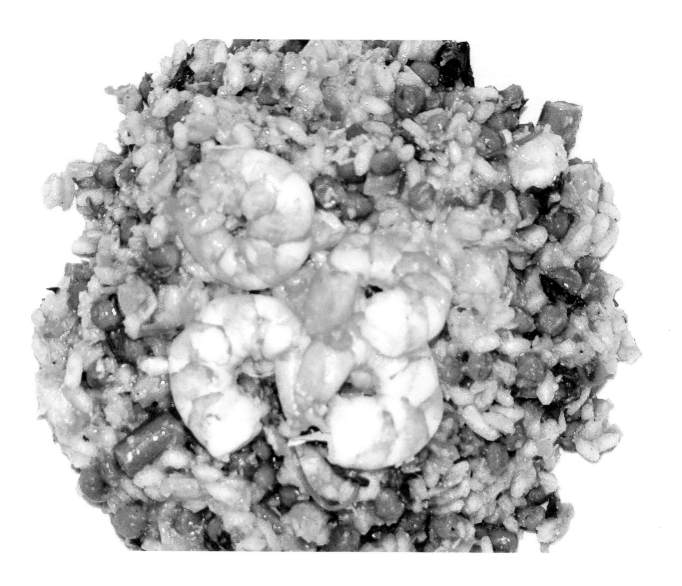

Recipe continued on next page.

Ingredients

8–10 parboiled spears of asparagus, diced (approx. 150g when cooked)

150g petit pois peas

50g butter

2 shallots

3 spring onions, chopped

1 garlic clove, chopped

Zest of 1 lemon (quite coarsely grated)

Juice ½ lemon

150g arborio / risotto rice (*tip: the better the quality of the rice, the better the dish!*)

600ml fish stock made by dissolving 1 fish stock pot / cube in warm water

1½ tbs grated parmesan cheese

120ml white wine (if you don't drink alcohol, substitute with the same volume of fish stock

60ml single cream

400g uncooked, good-quality Atlantic (cold-water) prawns (they are about 2cm long and can be bought frozen)

Salt and pepper

Handful parsley, coarsely chopped

Cooking instructions

1. Lightly parboil the asparagus and the peas, set aside.

2. Melt the butter in a deep, non-stick frying pan. Add the shallots, the sliced spring onions, garlic and the lemon zest and soften. Add pepper at this point. (*Tip: don't add salt just yet as the fish stock and the prawns can be quite salty, and you can overdo it.*) Add the lemon juice and stir into the arborio rice and buttery shallots. Stir the mixture well so the rice grains are coated in butter.

3. Over a medium heat, add the fish stock 100ml at a time, stirring constantly – this causes the rice to release the starch into the stock and thicken it. About halfway through, add the parmesan cheese, the wine (or additional stock) and then the single cream. Keep stirring!

4. Add the prawns and the parboiled asparagus and peas once the rice is almost cooked. For me, the rice grains should be separate but soft when done (i.e., al dente) – however, some people prefer a slight graininess to the rice; it's a matter of preference. Adjust the seasoning. Cook until the prawns are done and the whole risotto is a rich, creamy mixture with most of the fluid absorbed into the rice. Serve in pasta bowls and garnish with chopped parsley.

Stir-fried prawns

A crowd-pleaser – tasty and full of prawns and healthy vegetables!
This dish is very quick to cook but, as with many SE Asian dishes,
there is quite a lot of initial prepping and chopping!

Serves 2

Recipe continued on next page.

Ingredients

1 tsp black peppercorns

150g broccoli cut into florets

100g sugar snaps, string removed

2-3 tbs cooking oil

1 tsp sesame oil

3 spring onions, finely diagonally sliced (separate the white from the green parts)

2–3 inches grated fresh ginger root

1 red chilli, deseeded, chopped finely

2 garlic cloves, finely chopped

1 tbs dry white wine or rice wine (if you don't drink alcohol, leave this out)

1 tbs fish sauce

½ tsp shrimp paste – it's quite pungent!

1 tbs Japanese soy sauce

1 tbs sweet chilli sauce

3 medium-sized tomatoes, sliced

½ tsp palm sugar (or golden caster sugar)

Juice 1 lime

400g raw king prawns (crevettes), prepared and peeled

1 red pepper cut into thin strips

1 small tin water chestnuts, sliced into strips

100g bean bean sprouts

3 tbs roughly chopped roasted peanuts / cashews

120g fresh or dried rice or egg noodles – amount is dependent on appetites

Cooking instructions

1. Rapidly dry roast the peppercorns in a frying pan, and grind in a pestle and mortar or blitz in a food processor.

2. Lightly parboil the broccoli florets and the sugar snaps. Drain carefully.

3. Cook the noodles until al dente – add a tbs of oil to the water to prevent the noodles sticking together. Drain and set aside.

4. Peel the prawns. Add a little cooking oil to a frying pan and cook until nearly done. Cover with foil and set aside.

5. Put the cooking oils in a wok or deep-sided frying pan and stir-fry the white portion of the spring onions, the ginger, red chilli and garlic for 2 minutes. Add white / rice wine, ground peppercorns, fish sauce, shrimp paste (optional!), soy sauce, sweet chilli sauce, tomatoes, palm sugar and lime juice. Cover and cook for 3 minutes. Just before the end, add the pre-cooked prawns, red pepper, parboiled broccoli and sugar snaps, water chestnuts. Mix in the chopped roasted peanuts / cashews. Add the cooked noodles and mix with the fried vegetables. Add the bean sprouts at the last minute. Cook until the dish is hot.

6. Place portions into individual bowls and dress with the sliced green spring onions.

Prawn and coconut laksa

This is a delicious Malaysian dish which was one of the first dishes I tried when experimenting with fish cookery. I followed recipes very carefully in those early days, so I would like to acknowledge the great Delia Smith whose recipe this is based on. Her *Delia Collection: Fish* provided a great grounding in the principles of pescatarian cookery, and this gave me the confidence to try creating recipes for myself!

Serves 4

Ingredients

25–30 king prawns/crevettes (actual number depends on size of prawns)

500g fresh mussels

50g butternut squash, cubed

120g medium-thickness dried rice noodles

Laksa paste:

3 medium-sized red chillies, deseeded and chopped

2 tsp dried shrimp paste

4 medium-sized shallots, chopped

2 cloves garlic, finely chopped

2 tsp lemongrass puree (for suppliers see Store Cupboard, **page 12**)

2–3 inches fresh ginger root, peeled and chopped

2 tsp turmeric powder

50g unsalted peanuts

1–2 tbs cooking oil

400ml tin light coconut milk (*tip: try to use organic coconut milk if possible – it tastes much better*)

150g bean sprouts

Juice 1–1½ limes

2 tbs fish sauce

4 sprigs Thai basil, remove the leaves from the stalks

6–8 sprigs coriander – remove the stalks and chop the leaves

Cooking instructions

1. Peel the prawns and remove the black thread along the back of the fish. Scrub the mussels and cut off the beards. Discard any that are damaged or do not close when tapped.

2. Quickly fry the prawns in a little cooking oil. Remove before being completely cooked. Reserve on a plate. Cover with foil.

3. Parboil the butternut squash and then drain.

4. Cover the rice noodles with boiling water and soak for 8–10 minutes until soft. Drain in a sieve and rinse in cold water. Set aside.

5. Place all the paste ingredients in a food processor and blend until smooth.

6. Dry-roast the peanuts in a flat pan until golden. Chop roughly and then set aside on a plate.

7. Add oil to the same pan and then tip in the paste and cook for 2 minutes over a medium heat. Add the coconut milk and the cubed, parboiled butternut squash and cook gently until the squash is soft. Add the noodles, ¾ bean sprouts and the lime juice. Add the fish sauce, the prawns and the mussels. Cook for about 3–4 minutes until the mussels open. (*Tip: it's important not to overcook the ingredients which need to retain some crunchiness.*) Add the chopped Thai basil leaves and the rest of the bean sprouts and, finally, fold in the nuts.

8. Serve in bowls, making sure to evenly distribute the shellfish.

Salmon

Salmon is a highly versatile fish to cook. It has a delicate flavour and can be served very simply as a cold whole fish or as fillets, complemented with a wide variety of herbs, spices, sauces and cooking techniques.

I have selected a few of my favourite recipes which try to showcase this versatility.

Whole, cold poached salmon

There are numerous ways to cook salmon, but a whole cold poached salmon takes some beating for a centrepiece when producing a buffet for a large group. This is the way I cook this dish – many other recipes are available and I'm sure that you will find your own refinements and techniques.

Ingredients

Whole salmon (2.5–2.75kg), descaled, fins removed, head on or off according to preference and tail fin in a V shape

For the court bouillon:

2 lbs fresh fish bones/heads

2 onions, chopped

1 carrot, chopped

1 celery stick (or outer leaves of fennel), chopped

150ml white wine, or same volume of fish stock

Bouquet garni (comprising 3 sprigs lemon thyme, 6 sprigs parsley and 3 sprigs tarragon)

2 bay leaves

10 black peppercorns

1 litre of water

Salt and pepper

Aromatic seasonings:

1 chopped shallot

3 bay leaves

3 sprigs thyme (lemon thyme is particularly good)

6 sprigs parsley

3 sprigs dill

3 sprigs tarragon

1 lemon sliced thickly

½ fennel, sliced

Garnish:

1 cucumber, small bunch of red radishes

Cooking instructions

1. If you don't have a fish kettle, your fishmonger may hire them. If not, you will need a roasting tin which is sufficiently large to take the whole fish and deep enough for the poaching fluid to cover the salmon. If using a roasting tin, double line it with foil.

2. To make court bouillon: put all the listed ingredients into a pan and slowly bring to a simmer and cook for 30 minutes – remove any scum that forms. Strain the fluid and cool.

3. Season both sides and the cavity of the salmon with salt and pepper. Tuck the listed aromatic herbs into the cavity of the salmon.

4. Make a long cloth sling, or one made of several layers of tinfoil. Centre in the bottom of the roasting tin with the ends overhanging the short ends of the tin.

5. Place the sliced fennel and thickly sliced lemons on the sling so it protects the fish from burning when cooking on top of the stove.

6. Place the salmon into your poaching vessel on this sling, so you will be able to lift it when it is done.

Recipe continued on next page.

7. Cover the salmon with the court bouillon and add a generous pinch of salt and pepper. Cover with a lid or tinfoil. Slowly bring the fluid to a simmer on the top of the stove. (*Tip: put 2 heat sources on under the poaching vessel.*)

8. Once boiling, immediately turn off the heat, leaving the lid / tinfoil covering in position. Allow the fish to cool completely in the cooking fluid, and then lift out using the cotton / tinfoil sling.

9. When <u>completely</u> cold, use a knife to scrape off the skin and brown, fatty flesh from the top of the fish. Very carefully separate the two halves of the fish and then flip the top fillet onto a plate using a long spatula. Remove the central bones. Then clean and deskin the lower fillet. Reassemble the fish when this is done. To serve, cut the top fillet lengthways and cut portions from each side. Then do similarly with the lower fillet.

Presentation

Peel the cucumber and cut in half lengthways. Remove the seeds by running a teaspoon down the length of both the cucumber halves. Slice finely. Then slice the radishes. Place the radish down the centre of the fish and then arrange the cucumber slices as scales.

Serve with plain or tarragon mayonnaise.

Glazed, grilled/oven-baked salmon fillets with suggestions for enhancing flavours

Salmon fillets make a great fast supper dish, and the flavour can be jazzed up in different ways, as described below, which will keep the dishes interesting.

Recipe continued on next page.

Cooking instructions

For all these dishes, ideally try to take the salmon out of the fridge at least 15 minutes ahead of cooking to allow it to get to room temperature. This substantially reduces the cooking time and, therefore, the risk of overcooking and drying out the fish resulting in loss of texture. However, if you are in a rush and need to cook the fish immediately, just add a little extra cooking time to those suggested below which have assumed the fish is at room temperature.

Adding flavour to your salmon fillets...

Marinate the fish by placing the salmon fillets on a plate and squeezing on the juice of ½ lemon and season well with salt and pepper.

To add additional depth of flavour, brush the surface of the fillets with one of the following concentrated creams or pestos:

- **Asparagus cream:** to add a subtle flavour of asparagus to your fish, spread 1–2 tsp of the cream over each fillet before cooking (see Store Cupboard, **page 12**, to source this cream). Dot some pieces of butter on top and cook as described below. Serve with asparagus as a side dish.

- **Artichoke cream:** for a flavour of artichoke, spread 1–2 tsp of the artichoke cream over each fillet before cooking (see Store Cupboard, **page 12**, to source this cream). Dot some pieces of butter on top and cook as described below. Serve with sliced artichoke hearts – these can be bought in jars, either in oil (preferrable) or in natural juices. To serve, fry some finely chopped garlic and add about 1 tbs of sliced artichoke per person. Add a squeeze of lemon juice and heat quickly ahead of serving.

- **Truffle pesto:** this goes particularly well with salmon and gives a great added taste (see Store Cupboard, **page 12**, to source this pesto). Brush 1–2 tsp of the pesto over each fillet before cooking. Dot some pieces of butter on top and cook as described below. Serve with sliced mushrooms (porcini, Forestier or oyster) sautéed in a little butter with 1–2 tsp of the truffle pesto added. Add a little single cream and parmesan cheese. Before serving, sprinkle the salmon surface with roasted hazelnuts and place the mushrooms alongside the fillet.

- **Lemon hollandaise:** this provides a nice zingy lemon taste with minimal effort! Take 1 tbs of pre-made hollandaise sauce (see Store Cupboard, **page 12**, to source this sauce) and add the juice and zest of ½ lemon. Coat the fillets and dot some pieces of butter on top and scatter on finely chopped dill or tarragon. Cook as described below.

- **Miso and soy:** mix 2 tsp of good miso sauce with 1 tbs soy sauce, ½ tsp sesame seed oil and 1 tsp runny honey. Add 1 tbs of rice wine, 1 tsp of citrusy-flavoured yuzu juice (see the Store Cupboard, **page 12**, to source this) and a few flakes of roasted red chilli seeds. Brush this over the surface of the fillets and dot some pieces of butter on top and cook as described below.

To grill

1. Remove the grill pan from the oven and bring the grill up to 210°C. Line the grill tray with tinfoil and drizzle with olive oil to stop the fish sticking.

2. Place the salmon fillets, prepared as above on the foil, skin down. Grill the salmon for 4 minutes (the exact time depends on the thickness of the fish). Then flip over the fish and cook on the skin side for a further 2–3 minutes. The skin should be crispy. Check the core temperature of the fillets using a cooking thermometer – it should read between 48–50°C when done. If a thermometer is not available, you can use the techniques described in the section entitled 'Techniques for Successful Fish Cookery' to judge when the fillets are cooked (**See page 8**).

To bake

Preheat the oven to 210°C. Butter an open dish and place the salmon skin side down on it. Add any herbs/flavourings you are using on the upper surface (see above) and dot with knobs of butter (see the individual recipes). Cook for about 6 minutes, then check cooking progress every minute. If using a thermometer (recommended), the fish is done when the core internal temperature is 48–50°C, or you can use the techniques described in the section entitled 'Techniques for Successful Fish Cookery' to judge when the fillets are cooked (**See page 8**).

Salmon in filo pastry parcels

Salmon cooked 'en croûte' is usually made with puff pastry, but I prefer to substitute with filo pastry as it is lighter, and the cooking time is more predictable. This is a good entertaining dish as it can be prepared well ahead of time and then cooked when needed.

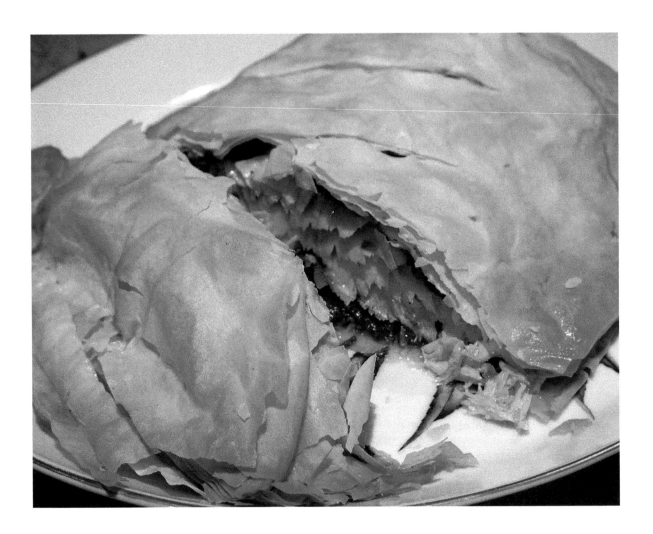

Ingredients

Salmon fillets (180–200g per person is a good size), remove the skin

Lemon juice

Salt and pepper

1 bag baby spinach leaves

½ tbs chopped roasted pine nuts per parcel

270g packet filo pastry (*tip: 1 box of pastry usually makes about 3 fish parcels*)

20g butter

Beaten egg and egg white

Cooking instructions

1. Marinate the salmon fillets for at least 15 minutes in lemon juice, season with salt and pepper. Then dry the salmon carefully between sheets of paper towel. (*Tip: change the paper a couple of times until the fish is dry, as this will help avoid a filo pastry fish parcel with the dreaded 'soggy bottom'!*)

2. Wilt the spinach, using as little water as possible, and when cooked, place in a sieve to drain – press as much moisture out as possible. Then, place it between sheets of paper towel to dry. Mix in the chopped roasted pine nuts. Season.

3. Prepare the filo pastry sheets as usual, brushing melted butter between each layer. I usually use 3–4 layers. Cut the filo so it will form a parcel round the salmon fillets. (*Tip: the top sheets need to be larger than the lower sheets so they will wrap round and hang over the sides of the fillet to make a well-sealed parcel. 1 box of filo sheets will make about 3 parcels.*)

4. Brush egg white over the inner surface of the lower layer of the parcel to seal the pastry. This helps to prevent the parcel getting soggy during cooking. Place sufficient spinach to cover the surface of the bottom layer of the pastry parcel and then place the salmon fillet on top. Put a few knobs of butter on the top surface of the salmon fillet and then cover with the filo pastry top. Seal down the pastry by painting the edges with butter. Trim the edges, leaving enough space for the salmon to expand a little during cooking.

5. With a sharp knife, cut 3 light slashes diagonally across the top of the parcel and brush the parcel thoroughly with beaten egg.

6. Butter a baking sheet and preheat it in the oven at 200°C. Place the salmon parcels on the hot sheet and cook for 10 minutes, then check on the cooking progress using a food thermometer. The core temperature inside the parcel will be 48–50°C when cooked and the pastry will be golden brown.

Serving suggestions and accompaniments

Asparagus with a dill hollandaise sauce is particularly good with this, accompanied by boiled baby potatoes finished with butter and chopped parsley.

Salmon and dill fishcakes

A posh version of fishcakes, which are good enough to serve for an informal meal with friends. They can be made ahead of time and then cooked when needed.

Makes 4–6 good-sized fishcakes, according to size

Ingredients

400g salmon fillet, skin removed

300g unsmoked haddock, skin removed

Juice of 1 lemon and zest of half of it

Salt and pepper

1 shallot, chopped

15g butter

½ small glass of wine You can omit this and use the same volume of fish stock made from a cube or ready-made stock pot)

1 bay leaf

A few sprigs of parsley, chopped

4 medium potatoes made into stiff mashed potato (I prefer red potatoes for their taste and texture)

4 spring onions, chopped

4 sprigs dill, chopped

2 tbs plain flour

1 beaten egg

3–4 tbs panko crumbs (if too course, use a rolling pin to make a finer crumb)

Cooking oil

Cooking instructions

1. Marinate the fish in ½ lemon juice and season with salt and pepper for at least 15 minutes.

2. Preheat the oven to 200°C.

3. In a heavy-based frying pan, fry the shallot in butter until golden brown, and then add the wine / fish stock, a bay leaf, chopped parsley and seasoning. Add the fish and cook for about 8 minutes until just cooked. Cool.

4. Flake the fish into the mashed potato and add the chopped spring onions, dill and the remaining lemon juice and zest of ½ lemon.

5. Shape the fish and potato mixture onto equal sized balls (4–6 depending on size) and then gently flatten to form fishcakes. Dust with plain flour, then brush with beaten egg and finally roll in panko crumbs – press lightly to ensure the crumbs adhere to the surface of the fishcakes.

6. Heat the cooking oil in a heavy-based, non-stick, ovenproof frying pan and brown the fishcakes on both sides. If they are getting overly brown on the outside but are not sufficiently cooked inside, transfer the whole pan to the oven to finish off (check the pan can withstand the high temperatures). Check regularly that they are not burning. Using a thermometer, the core temperature should be 48–50°C when cooked. Remember to use oven gloves when removing the pan from the oven.

Serving suggestions and accompaniments

Serve with a dill sauce: into 1 small pot of thick crème fraîche, add 1 very finely chopped garlic clove, juice ½ lemon, dill (amount depends on how much you like this taste!), salt and pepper to season. Mix thoroughly.

Salmon fillets in champagne sauce

This is a special-occasion dish and a good solution if you have some champagne left over that has gone a little flat… if that doesn't seem a likely scenario, then this recipe works well with prosecco! This dish was inspired by a Delia Smith recipe – she was a huge inspiration to me during my early cooking days. If you don't drink alcohol, then this recipe might not be for you as the champagne is a prominent ingredient.

Serves 2

Ingredients

2 x 180–200g salmon fillets

Juice ½ lemon

Salt and pepper

40g butter for frying

1 large shallot, finely chopped

120ml champagne or prosecco

8 sprigs dill, destalked and chopped

15g plain flour

Small carton double cream

10g grated parmesan cheese

Salmon caviar to garnish

Cooking instructions

1. Marinate the salmon fillets in the juice of ½ lemon for at least 15 minutes, and season with salt and pepper. Carefully dry the fish between sheets of paper towel. Warm the oven to 100°C.

2. Melt half of the butter and cook the chopped shallot for 2–3 minutes until soft and golden but not browned. Put to one side.

3. Generously butter a non-stick frying pan. Add the salmon fillets when hot. Pour champagne/prosecco over the fillets – it may foam. Add half the chopped dill. Bring to a simmer over a medium heat. Baste the fish with the champagne/prosecco several times. Place a lid on the pan and cook for 5 minutes.

4. Test if sufficiently cooked (the fish should not be completely cooked at this point): the core temperature should be 40–45°C using a cooking thermometer, or insert a sharp knife into the thickest part of the fillet. If the flesh is beginning to flake, but still has some translucency in the middle, it is cooked sufficiently at this point. It should not, however, look raw. When the salmon is removed from the pan, place it on a plate, cover with foil and keep warm in the gently warmed oven (see above).

5. Mix the flour into the buttery shallots, stir in and cook for 1–2 minutes. Add the warm salmon poaching fluid and then blend in sufficient double cream to make a rich coating consistency sauce, whisking vigorously. Add the rest of the chopped dill, plus the grated parmesan cheese. Gradually bring to a simmer and cook for 1 minute. (*Tip: loosen the sauce with more of the poaching fluid and double cream as needed.*) Adjust seasoning. Sieve the sauce.

Serving suggestions and accompaniments

Plate up the salmon fillets and spoon the sauce around the fish. Garnish with sprigs of dill, pan-fried king prawn or red salmon caviar. Boiled, buttered baby potatoes and asparagus are good accompaniments.

Half side of salmon, baked in the oven

This is quite an easy dish to cook. It looks impressive and can be served hot or cold. For this recipe, it is assumed the fish will be served cold.

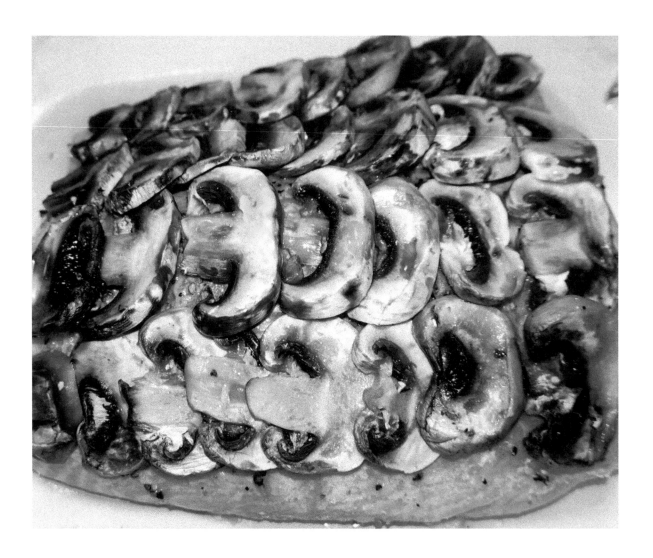

Ingredients

Half side of salmon with the skin removed (*tip: to calculate the weight of salmon fillet you need where the salmon is a main dish, multiply the number of guests by appox. 200g fish each*)

Salt and pepper

Juice and zest of 1 lemon

30g butter

Sprigs of lemon thyme, flat parsley and dill, chopped

75ml white wine (if you don't drink alcohol substitute with fish stock)

200–300g button mushrooms

Cooking instructions

1. Bring the salmon fillet up to room temperature and marinate in the juice of a lemon and salt and pepper seasoning for at least 15 minutes. Dry the salmon on a paper towel.

2. Place a baking sheet in the oven and heat to 200°C.

3. Generously butter the inner surface of a large sheet of tinfoil. Then cover the surface with the finely chopped lemon thyme, flat parsley, dill and seasoning. Lay the salmon on it and grate the zest of 1 lemon over the fish and squeeze on the juice. Brush the surface of the fish with a generous amount of melted butter.

4. Slice enough small white mushrooms to cover the surface of the fish (see photo).

5. Wrap the salmon in a foil parcel. Before sealing, pour over a small glass of white wine or fish stock (see above). Seal the parcel, making sure that the fluids do not leak. Place the fish on the preheated baking tray.

6. Cook for 12–15 minutes at 180°C and then check how the cooking is progressing: this can be judged by opening the parcel and inserting a cooking thermometer into the thickest part of the fillet and it will be done if between 48–52°C. Or, insert a sharp knife between the fish flakes. If the flesh is beginning to flake, but still has a little translucency in the middle, it is done. If not done, continue cooking and check progress every 1 minute.

7. When done, and to prevent further cooking, open the foil parcel immediately. Carefully place the salmon onto another tray.

Serving suggestions and accompaniments

Try serving with a salad with either a dill mayonnaise sauce (mayonnaise blitzed with garlic, spring onion, dill and seasoning) or an avocado sauce (crème fraiche, blitzed with a ripe avocado, garlic, lemon zest and seasoning). Add a ¼ tsp of cider vinegar and lemon juice to either sauce to sharpen their taste.

Hot smoked and fresh salmon and asparagus quiche

Quiche comes in many flavours and presentations. I love traditional Quiche Lorraine,
but keeping to our fish theme, making a pescatarian version with two varieties
of salmon is tasty and different!

Serves 6

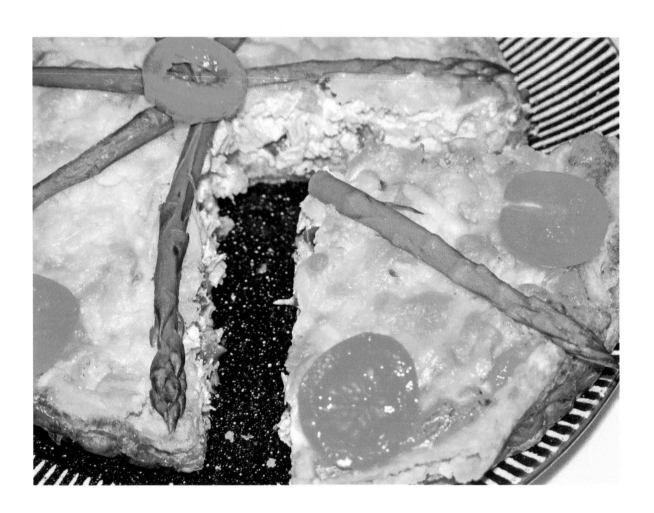

Ingredients

320g good-quality ready-made shortcrust pastry

300g fresh salmon fillets, skinned

3 sprigs of dill, chopped

25g butter

150g hot smoked salmon fillet

100g asparagus, parboiled

1 large shallot, finely chopped

2–3 inner leaves of fresh fennel, sliced

3 eggs

50ml whole milk

200ml double cream

Zest of 1 lemon

Juice of ½ lemon

2–3 sprigs of fresh tarragon or dill, chopped

Salt and pepper

Grated cheddar cheese to sprinkle on top of quiche

4–5 small tomatoes, halved

Cooking instructions

1. Take the pastry out of the fridge 30 minutes before use.

2. Preheat the oven to 180°C.

3. Butter and line a 23cm / 9-inch loose-bottomed quiche tin with non-stick baking parchment. Line with shortcrust pastry, making sure that the pastry is at least ½ an inch above the top of the flan dish. Prick the base and place on a baking tray. Cover with a circle of greaseproof paper and weight it down with baking beans/pasta. Cook in a preheated oven at 180°C for 15 minutes. Remove the beans and the greaseproof paper and place the pastry case back in the oven to cook through and form a crisp base (approx. 10 minutes).

4. To cook the fresh salmon fillet, remove the skin and place on buttered foil. Season with salt and pepper and scatter on the chopped dill. Finish with 15g butter cut into small pieces. Wrap the salmon in the foil and cook for 8 minutes in the oven at 200°C. Allow to cool and then flake into small pieces.

5. Flake the hot smoked salmon fillets.

6. Drain the parboiled asparagus and cut into small pieces.

7. Melt the remaining butter in a pan and add the chopped shallot and sliced fennel. Cook until soft and golden.

8. To make the egg filling: beat the 3 eggs and pour in the double cream. Add the whole milk. Add the lemon juice and zest and either chopped tarragon or dill. Season with salt and pepper.

Recipe continued on next page.

9. To prepare the quiche, place a layer of the sautéed shallot and fennel at the bottom of the flan dish. Then add the flaked salmon. Check seasoning and adjust as needed. Carefully pour in the egg/cream mix. Finish by lightly covering the top with grated cheddar cheese. Decorate with the halved, small tomatoes.

10. Bake for 40 minutes at 180°C or until the centre is just set and the top is golden brown. Cool before serving and neaten off the top edge of the quiche with a knife when the pastry is cold. This can be prepared ahead of time as the dish improves with standing.

Salmon coulibiac

A Russian dish in origin and adopted by the French. It has been adapted in many ways and this is my version. It is a great take on a fish pie and works well on a buffet as it can be prepared in advance, looks appetising and is easy to serve.

Serves 4

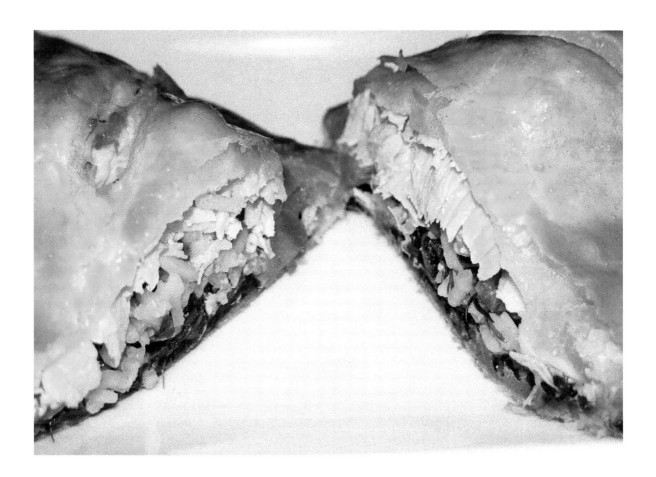

Recipe continued on next page.

Ingredients

50g butter

100g basmati rice

200ml fish stock – place ½ a Knorr fish cube or concentrated fish stock pot in warm water or make stock from fish bones

250g bag of spinach

600-700g salmon fillet, whole or as individual fillets, skinned

Salt and pepper

2 shallots, chopped

2 tbs dill, chopped

2 tbs parsley, chopped

½ lemon zest

2 tbs lemon juice

2x320g packets of all-butter ready-rolled puff pastry (this takes more pastry than you might think)

4 medium-sized hard-boiled eggs (boiled for 8 minutes, shelled, and roughly chopped)

1 additional egg beaten for brushing over the pastry

Cooking instructions

1. Melt half the butter (25g) in a pan and stir in the rice. Add the fish stock and bring to the boil. Add a little salt. Stir well and simmer for 15 minutes or until cooked and the stock has been absorbed. Drain and allow to cool.

2. Wilt the spinach and then drain very thoroughly. Dry on 2–3 layers of paper towel.

3. Preheat oven to 180°C. Line a baking sheet with buttered foil. Lay the salmon on it and brush with melted butter. Season, and wrap the fish in the foil and place in oven for 8 minutes (it only needs to partly cook at this point). Open the foil and allow to cool.

4. Use the rest of the butter to sweat the chopped shallots for 5 minutes and then add ½ the dill and ½ tbs parsley. Stir in the lemon zest and the juice. Cool.

5. Break the salmon up into large flakes and fold in the chopped hard-boiled eggs, the remaining dill and ½ tbs parsley. Season.

6. Combine the rice with the shallots and the rest of the parsley (1 tbs).

7. Roll the puff pastry into a 30cm square. Cut into 2 lengths, one wider than the other. (*Tip: you may be able to get this out of 1 packet of pastry – however, I always have another at the ready!*)

8. Brush the baking sheet with melted butter and lay the narrower strip of pastry on it. Spoon ½ the rice along the centre of the pastry strip, leaving a 2cm margin round the edge. Spread the well drained, wilted spinach over the rice. Spoon the salmon and egg mix onto the rice. Then, mould on another rice layer, lightly pressing it into the layer below. (*Tip: don't overfill the pie as it will crack open when cooking.*)

9. Brush the margins of the pastry with beaten egg and place on the other larger piece of pastry. Press the pastry edges together, trim any excess, feather the edges and crimp. Make several light diagonal slashes across the top of the pie and brush the pastry with beaten egg and cook for 20–25 minutes at 180°C until the parcel is golden brown (internal temperature should be 48–50°C). Rest for 10 minutes before serving.

10. The coulibiac eats well when cold.

Salmon, haddock and prawn fish pie

There are as many delicious recipes for fish pie as there are enthusiastic fish cooks! So, with some trepidation, I thought that I would give you my take on a firm family favourite, which you can weigh up in comparison with your own fish pie recipe! I hope that you like it!

Serves 4–6 depending on portion size

164

Ingredients

300g salmon fillets

300g unsmoked haddock/cod, skin removed

150–200g bag good-quality frozen king prawns,
    Drain, dry and cut in half crossways

½ lemon juice

Salt and pepper

300ml full-fat milk

1 leek, finely sliced

2 dried bay leaves

1 fish stock cube/concentrated stock pot

40g butter

40g plain flour, plus an additional 2 tbs to coat the fish

50ml single cream

50ml white wine (optional)

Handful parsley, chopped

150g tinned sweetcorn, drained

150g frozen petit pois, thawed, drained

Zest 1 lemon

2 tsp Dijon mustard

100g grated mature cheddar

Mashed potato to cover your pie dish (*tip: I prefer red potatoes*)

Cooking instructions

1. Dice the fish and the prawns. Marinate in lemon juice and salt and pepper seasoning for at least 15 minutes.

2. Infuse full-fat milk with the finely chopped leek, dried bay leaves and a crumbled fish stock cube/fish stock pot. Bring to simmering point very slowly. If you have time, leave the mix to cool, the flavours will be more intense.

3. Make the bechamel sauce: melt 40g butter in a saucepan and mix in 40g plain flour. Cook briskly for 1–2 minutes. Add the warm milk infusion (remove the bay leaves), single cream and the white wine (optional) to the butter/flour mix and bring to the boil slowly. (*Tip: always add warm fluids to a roux to avoid lumps.*) The consistency needs to be thicker than a typical white sauce as the fish will generate juices while cooking and thin it. Add chopped parsley, sweetcorn, the petit pois peas, lemon zest, Dijon mustard and 50g grated cheese. Simmer, stirring all the time. Adjust seasoning.

4. Place the diced fish/prawns in a plastic bag and add 2 tbs seasoned plain flour. Shake the bag to lightly, but evenly, to coat the fish with the flour. (*Tip: this will help prevent the fish juices causing a thin, sloppy sauce.*) Place the fish in a buttered pie dish and pour on the sauce. Top with mashed potatoes and sprinkle on the remaining grated cheese (you may need more cheese if your pie dish is wide). Cook for 30 minutes at 180°C. If using a cooking thermometer, the temperature at the centre of the pie should be 50°C.

Trout and toasted flaked almonds

Trout is a freshwater fish, and member of the salmon family.
It has a delicate texture and an almost nutty taste. Careful cooking can
accentuate its good points, making it a great everyday dish.

Serves 2

Ingredients

1 large trout, filleted

Juice ½ lemon

Salt and pepper

1 tbs olive oil

1tsp asparagus puree/cream (for suppliers see Store
Cupboard, **page 12**)

15g butter

Roasted flaked almonds

Salt and pepper

Cooking instructions

1. Marinate the trout fillets for at least 15 minutes in the lemon juice and season with salt and pepper. Pat dry with paper towel.

2. Remove the grill tray and heat the grill to 210°C.

3. Line the grill rack with tinfoil. Drizzle with olive oil to stop the fillets sticking. Lay out the fish fillets. To add an extra depth of taste, brush 1 tsp of the asparagus cream on the surface of each of the trout fillets. Drizzle on some more olive oil over the fish fillets or add some knobs of butter. Add a little more salt and pepper.

4. Cook for 5 minutes under the grill. After this time, shake on the roasted flaked almonds. Return the fish to cook for 1 minute or until cooked.

Serving suggestions and accompaniments

Serve with grilled asparagus. Take a bunch of asparagus and cut to an equal length. Parboil in salt water for 1 minute if thin stems and for up to 3 minutes for thicker ones. Heat a ridged griddle pan and glaze with olive oil. When smoking hot, place the asparagus on the hot surface and cook until the side of the asparagus in contact with the skillet chars slightly. Turn the asparagus spears over and cook on the other side. This striped effect looks quite professional and gives the vegetable a nice, barbecued taste.

Alternatively, consider butter bean puree. Drain a can of butter beans. Cook in a little of the fluid they come in plus olive oil, a little garlic, parsley and thyme. Once cooked, pop the beans out of their rather tough outer skins. Blitz into a puree and add a little cream to loosen. Adjust the seasoning, adding a little nutmeg and lemon juice to sharpen the taste.

Steamed trout with ginger and spring onions

A delicious SE Asian take on the preparation of trout. You will need a bamboo steamer or a metal fan steamer to cook this dish. The latter expands to fit across a regular saucepan half full of boiling water – try to buy one made in stainless steel. (*Tip: I prefer the fan steamers as you can lay out a larger fish than in the bamboo baskets.*) Both are available online – for suppliers see Store Cupboard, **page 12**.

Serves 2

Ingredients

1 large trout, filleted

Juice ½ lime

Salt and pepper

½ tsp roasted chilli seeds

½ tbs soy sauce

2 tsp sesame oil

Handful coriander, chopped

To steam the fish:

½ tsp roasted chilli seeds

2 inches fresh ginger root, peeled and sliced very fine

1 red chilli, chopped finely

4 spring onions, sliced diagonally

1 garlic clove, diced very small

3–4 sprigs of Thai basil, remove the leaves from the stalks and chop

1 tsp fish sauce

Zest of 1 lime

To make the sauce:

1 tsp grated fresh ginger

½ garlic clove, diced

3 tbs Japanese soy sauce

3 tbs brown rice wine or a dry white wine, or non-alcoholic substitute

1 tsp sesame seed oil

½ tsp palm sugar or honey – simmer for 5 minutes

Coriander leaves to garnish

Cooking instructions

1. Marinate the fish fillets in the lime juice for at least 15 minutes. Pat dry with a paper towel. Drizzle on the soy sauce and sesame seed oil. Season with salt, pepper and the roasted chilli seeds. Dry on paper towel.

2. Place all the ingredients to steam the fish in a bowl and mix. Bring a pan of water to a rolling boil. Line the steamer with the foil and place it on top of the pan of boiling water, ensuring there is a generous gap between the water level and the bottom of the steamer. Place half the mixture on the surface of the steamer and lay the trout fillets on top. Season and splash the surface of the fish with a little soy sauce and sesame oil. Place the rest of the ingredients on top. Loosely cover with tinfoil, or the lid if using a bamboo steamer. Steam the fish for 6–8 minutes or until cooked.

3. To make the sauce: place the ingredients listed above into a small saucepan and simmer for 3–5 minutes. Pour over the fillets when served. Garnish with chopped coriander leaves.

Serving suggestions and accompaniments

Serve with jasmine rice, baby corn on the cob and mangetout with petit pois.

Scallops

Scallops are very popular and, when carefully cooked, they have a rich, delicately sweet flavour. To keep their succulent taste and moist texture, it is important not to overcook them.

Scallops with minted pea puree

This is a classic scallop dish, and the pea puree really complements the sweetness of the shellfish. Better still, it's fast to prepare! Always try to get fresh 'dry scallops' for this dish – if they have sat in water, they will absorb it and will not caramelise when pan-fried.
(*Tip: personally, I prefer to use scallops with the red roe attached as it tastes delicious, but remove it if you don't like it.*)

Serves 2 for a main dish

Ingredients

8 good-sized scallops – preferably fresh, but frozen scallops will work too

Juice ½ lemon

Salt and pepper

½ tsp roasted chilli seeds

25g butter

1 shallot, finely chopped

1 tbs pancetta

250g minted, frozen petit pois

Leaves from 2 sprigs of mint

2 tbs water

1–2 tbs single cream

3–4 tbs cooking oil

Cooking instructions

1. Take the scallops out of the fridge and marinate in lemon juice, salt, pepper and the roasted chilli seeds for 15 minutes. Carefully dry between sheets of paper towel. (*Tip: it is important to thoroughly dry the scallops before cooking, otherwise they will boil rather than pan-fry and will not caramelise on the outside surface. If you need to dry further, dust the scallops very lightly with plain flour to absorb the excess moisture.*)

2. To make the pea puree, melt the butter in a saucepan and add the chopped shallot. Fry until soft. Add the pancetta and cook until golden. Add the frozen peas and stir into the shallot and pancetta mix. Add the mint and water and bring to the boil and continue to boil for 2–3 minutes. Drain and cool. Remove the mint. Place in a food processor and blitz for 1–2 minutes until the pea puree is smooth. Loosen with 2 tbs single cream if the puree is too thick. (*Tip: for special occasions, pass the puree through a fine sieve to ensure it is velvety smooth.*) Adjust seasoning. This will stand in the fridge overnight if you need to prepare ahead of serving.

3. Heat a heavy-bottomed frying pan and add the cooking oil. When sizzling, add the scallops. (*Tip: put the large ones in first so they cook for a little longer.*) They will cook very fast. Fry for about 1½–2 minutes on one side and 1 minute on the other. The surface of the scallops should be golden brown and caramelised. The centre of the scallops should be juicy and have the appearance of mother-of-pearl. If using a cooking thermometer, the internal temperature should be 45°C.

Serving suggestions and accompaniments

Place 2 tbs of the pea puree onto the serving plate and, using the back of the spoon, draw it out into an attractive swirl. Place the scallops along the swirl. Serve with asparagus spears and tender green French beans.

Coquille St. Jacques (scallops)

This is a traditional French way of cooking scallops (coquille) – delicious, delicate and yummy. It's a little fiddlier than some dishes I've described but well worth the effort. This dish looks best served in real scallop shells. (*Tip: these can be sourced in sets of eight shells online – for suppliers, see Store Cupboard,* **page 12**).

Serves 2

Ingredients

6 scallops with the roe attached

Juice ½ lemon

Salt and pepper

For mashed potatoes:

300g red potatoes, peeled

30g butter

For scallop sauce:

20g butter

1 large shallot, finely chopped

2 small tender leeks, finely chopped

1 tbs plain flour

100ml single cream

50ml white wine, or equivalent volume of fish stock

20g grated Comté/gruyere cheese

Cooking instructions

1. Marinate the scallops for 15 minutes in juice ½ lemon and season with salt and pepper. Then, dry carefully on a paper towel. Next, detach the red roe and cut the scallops in half horizontally and season. Dry carefully on paper towel when marinated.

2. Cook the potatoes in salted water until soft. Mash thoroughly to avoid any lumps. Add the butter to ensure the mix is rich. It needs to be quite stiff. Season.

3. Heat the oven to 180°C fan and the grill to 200°C.

4. Soften the shallots and leeks in the butter. Add the flour and cook for 1 minute, stirring constantly. Add the cream and then the white wine/or fish stock (*tip: warm the liquids first to prevent lumping*) and bring to the boil. Stir all the time. Cook for 1–2 minutes. Season with salt and pepper and add half the grated cheese.

5. Brush the inside surface of the scallop shells/gratin serving dishes with olive oil. Spoon on half the shallot and leek sauce and then arrange the sliced scallops and the roe on top. Spoon the rest of the sauce on top. Build up the mashed potato round the sides of the shells/gratin dishes. (*Tip: this looks best if piped around the edge for a special occasion.*) Scatter on the rest of the grated cheese over the top. Place onto a baking tray. (*Tip: the scallop shells will be more stable during cooking if you place a scoop of mashed potato onto the baking tray for each shell and stand the shells on this.*) Bake for about 10 minutes. Finish under the grill until the cheese and potatoes are golden brown. If you are using a cooking thermometer, the core temperature of the dish when cooked should be 45–48°C.

Serving suggestions and accompaniments

Serve with a side dish of very fine, tender green beans tossed in a little butter.

See next page for photograph of completed dish.

Dover Sole

This is an exceptionally delicious, oval-shaped flatfish that lives on the seabed. It has a firm texture and, if freshly caught, it should be allowed to 'relax' in the fridge for a couple of days before cooking. I personally love this fish and I have provided one classic way to prepare it – sole meunière – and one more complex recipe for contrast. The skin cannot be eaten and should be removed on both sides – if possible, ask your fishmonger to do this as it is quite tricky, and you don't want to damage the flesh below. Enjoy!

Sole meunière

This is a classic Dover Sole dish, and if the fish is in prime condition, to my mind its simplicity showcases the fish to perfection. It's a case of 'less is more'! Many years ago, when I first became interested in food and cooking, I had my first sole meunière, and I can still clearly recall the wonderful taste – and the delicious glass of Meursault which went with it!

Serves 2

Ingredients

Allow 1 fish per person – either filleted or cooked on the bone. My preference is on the bone, with the skin on both sides and the fins removed. (*Tip: if you are an enthusiastic fish cook, and you have asked for the fish to be filleted, then ask for the bones – bag them up and put them in the freezer as they will make excellent fish stock!*)

Juice 1 lemon

Salt and pepper

A little plain flour

Cooking oil for pan-frying

40g butter

Cooking instructions

1. Marinate the fish for at least 15 minutes in half the lemon juice and season with salt and pepper.

2. If cooking more fish than you have frying pans, then heat the oven to a low temperature (100°C).

3. Dry the fish carefully between sheets of paper towel. (*Tip: the drier the flesh the more caramelised it will be when pan-fried.*) Carefully dust the fish all over with seasoned plain flour. Shake off the excess.

4. Cook the fish in a large, heavy-bottomed, non-stick frying pan. I recommend frying the fish in a high-quality, tasteless cooking oil, such as sunflower oil. Cook the fish for 2–3 minutes each side until it is golden brown. Then, add a generous knob of butter and quickly baste the fish for a further ½–1 minute.

5. If cooking the fish in batches, slightly undercook the fish, then cover it loosely with foil and place in the oven preheated to a low temperature. (*Tip: it is important to avoid the fish continuing to cook.*)

6. When all the fish are cooked, take a clean pan, melt the remaining butter and heat to the point that it just turns brown, add the rest of the lemon juice and pour over the fish.

Serving suggestion and accompaniments

To avoid the accompanying vegetables getting mixed up with the fish bones on the main plate, I use a side dish for each place setting so diners can put their vegetables on these.

Sole Veronique

Hands up, this is a rather fiddly dish – and quite difficult to execute perfectly.
However, when cooked well, it is delicious and looks impressive.

Serves 4

Ingredients

2 Dover sole – filleted, dark and the white skin removed

Juice ½ lemon

Salt and pepper

Fine string for tying the fish rolls

2–3 small new potatoes per person

20g butter

2–3 spring onions, chopped

½ celery stick, chopped

Herbs: 1 tbs fresh tarragon, 2–3 springs lemon thyme, 2 tbs parsley, chopped.

1 tbs plain flour

100ml white wine (*tip: choose a sweetish wine or use the equivalent amount of fish stock and add to the final volume of fish stock in the next line.*)

150ml fish stock – use a fish cube or home-made fish stock)

40g button mushrooms, sliced

100ml single cream

75g green grapes, halved and deseeded

Chopped parsley and tarragon for garnish

Cooking instructions

1. Marinate the fillets in lemon juice, salt and pepper for at least 15 minutes. Then, carefully dry on paper towel.

2. Divide each fillet in half lengthways – there will be 8 fillets in all. Roll up the fillets and secure with fine string – this is the fiddly bit!

3. Boil the new potatoes until just cooked.

4. Melt the butter in a frying pan and quickly fry the spring onions, celery, tarragon, lemon thyme and parsley. Add the plain flour and cook for 2–3 minutes. Add the white wine and fish stock (see note above if you do not drink wine). Cook until the sauce has thickened. (*Tip: you need a light coating consistency – add a little stock if you need to thin the sauce.*) Bring the sauce to a simmer point. Add the fish parcels to the sauce and add the sliced mushrooms.

5. Poach the fish rolls for 4–5 minutes (depends on size / thickness of the fish parcels). If using a cooking thermometer, the centre of the rolls should be 48°C. Remove the fillets and place on a lightly warmed plate. (*Tip: put the plate over a pan of steaming hot water – but not boiling or the fish will cook.*) Cover with foil. Quickly add the single cream to the sauce and whisk vigorously. The sauce should not be too thick. Sieve the sauce and then add the halved green grapes and let them heat through.

6. To serve, use a slotted spoon to put the fish rolls on a warmed serving plate. Remove the string around them and pour on the sauce. Arrange the mushrooms and new potatoes, finish with fresh chopped parsley and tarragon. Scatter over the green grapes.

Turbot

This might be the last of the fish sections in this book, but this is definitely deserving of your attention! Turbot is said to be the king of the culinary fish world.

Turbot is a round-shaped flatfish which has rather knobbly dark skin and a white underbelly. The flesh is pearly white and very delicious. It can grow to a large size when it is sold as steaks, but smaller fish are available which can be conveniently prepared as individual fillets.

I tend to use turbot for special occasions when I take particular care with its preparation and cooking.

Pan-fried turbot with lobster sauce

This is a delicious dish I have used for special occasions such as Christmas lunch,
for those who would prefer a pescatarian option to roast Turkey – myself included!

Serves 2

Ingredients

For garnish:

320g all butter ready-made puff pastry

1 beaten egg

For the stock:

The shell of a cooked good-sized lobster (see section 'For the fish' for instructions about cooking the lobster)

1 shallot, chopped

1 garlic clove, chopped

2–3 leaves of fresh fennel, chopped

1 stick celery, chopped

1 carrot, chopped

3 strips of orange peel with the white pith removed

1 star anise

2 sprigs of lemon thyme and parsley, chopped

2 bay leaves

500ml water

For the sauce:

20g butter

20g plain flour

50ml white wine. Or substitute the same volume of fish stock if you do not drink wine

2 tbs brandy. Omit if you do not drink alcohol

3–4 tbs double cream

½ tsp English mustard

2 tsp good-quality tomato puree

2 tbs grated gruyere cheese

Salt and pepper

For the fish:

Either 2 turbot fillets, or if taken from a larger fish, 2 steaks (*tip: ask for the skin to be removed*)

Flesh of the lobster (cooked)

Juice 1 lemon

Salt and pepper

1 tbs seasoned plain flour

Cooking oil for pan-frying

20g butter

For the spinach:

250g baby spinach

2 tbs hot water

Knob butter

For the mushrooms:

2 oyster mushrooms, halved

20g butter

2 sprigs lemon thyme, remove leaves from stems

Cooking instructions

1. Make your puff pastry garnish ahead of time. Use all-butter, pre-rolled puff pastry and, using a pastry cutter or a paper template you have made, cut a suitable pastry shape for the occasion, e.g. a fish or Christmas tree if this is for a Christmas menu. Brush with beaten egg and place on a buttered baking tray and cook in the oven at 180°C until golden.

Recipe continued on next page.

2. Now, make your stock. Take the lobster meat from the body and claws and reserve. Place the shell in a large pan, plus some prawn shells if you have kept any in the deep freeze from a previous dish. Then, place the chopped shallot, garlic clove, fresh fennel, celery, carrot and the strips of orange peel in a pan, together with the star anise, sprigs of thyme, parsley and bay leaves. Add the water. Bring slowly to a simmer and skim off any scum. Then, continue to cook for 30 minutes. Allow to cool and then strain, keeping the stock and throwing away the residue left in the strainer. Reduce the stock by a third so it concentrates.

3. Melt the butter needed for the sauce and tip in the flour, stir thoroughly and cook for 2 minutes. Then, slowly add the warm stock and the white wine (if using)/fish stock, beating the sauce continuously. (*Tip: if the stock is warm, it will not lump when beaten into the butter and flour roux.*) Add the brandy (if using), double cream, English mustard, tomato puree and grated gruyere cheese. Mix in and then adjust the seasoning. (*Tip: it is best to season the sauce after it has concentrated to avoid it becoming too salty.*) The consistency of the sauce should coat the back of a spoon but not be too thick. The sauce can be rested at this point.

4. Start preparing your fish. Remove from the fridge and marinade for at least 15 minutes in the juice of a lemon and salt and pepper.

5. Now, place your spinach into a pan and pour in the hot water. Wilt and then drain carefully to remove as much of the cooking water as possible. Dry on paper towel. Season and stir in a knob of butter.

6. Lightly pan-fry the mushrooms in butter with 1 or 2 sprigs of thyme. Season and drain.

7. Slice the lobster meat ahead of cooking the turbot.

8. To pan-fry the fish, dry carefully between sheets of paper towel. (*Tip: this is important – if the fish is wet, it will boil and will not caramelise when pan-fried.*) Dust the fish surfaces with lightly seasoned plain flour. Pan-fry the fish in a heavy-bottomed, non-stick frying pan, using cooking oil. Cook for 2–3 minutes on either side until the fillets are golden brown. Add the butter just before cooking is complete and baste the fish – this gives a nice rich taste.

9. 1 minute before the fish is cooked, quickly heat the sliced lobster meat in a little butter before serving – see below.

Serving suggestions and accompaniments

Firstly, lay out a bed of spinach on your serving plate, then place the turbot on top. Arrange the sliced lobster on the dish and decorate the plate with mushrooms and the puff pastry decoration. Spoon on the lobster sauce around the fish. (*Tip: don't overdo this – less is more when plating up. Hand round the remaining sauce at the table. However, if there is any left, keep it in the freezer as lobster sauce can liven up any fish dish in the future!*)

Serve with asparagus and sauté potatoes. (*Tip: supermarkets sell prepared sauté potatoes which are flash cooked at home in a hot oven. They are crispy and delicious – just take care they don't overcook as they brown very quickly.*)

Index

Cook's notes